DOG TRAINING
IN A
Weekend

DOG TRAINING
IN A
Weekend

The easy way to train your dog

Caroline Davis • Keith Davis

hamlyn

First published in Great Britain in 2003 by
Hamlyn, a division of Octopus Publishing Group Ltd
2–4 Heron Quays, London E14 4JP

ISBN 0 600 60768 2

A CIP catalogue record for this book is available from
the British Library

Printed in China

10 9 8 7 6 5 4 3 2 1

contents

BEFORE THE WEEKEND: 8 key elements

Given a fit, healthy adult dog of average intelligence (a Labrador Retriever for example) with no behavioural hang-ups, you can expect to achieve an obedience requirement described in the 'Weekend obedience training' section in one weekend – and there's a good chance of achieving more.

To do this, you will have to set aside approximately eight 15-minute sessions per day. Continually reinforce what you have initially taught throughout the week while out on regular exercise, or in ordinary playtime in the garden.

Many people, young and old alike, regard their dog as part of the family.

Some areas of obedience training complement others. For example, once you have taught your dog to sit, lying down and rolling over should come easily to him.

Bear in mind that some areas will need groundwork before you can achieve the response you desire. For example, a dog that doesn't know his name is not likely to come to you when you call him.

While we should not attribute human characteristics to dogs (anthropomorphism), they are intelligent enough to understand and then perform many actions, provided these actions are requested in a way that dogs find rewarding.

With this principle in mind, owners have to be clever, too, and find a way of training their dogs that works quickly and effectively. This book explains how to achieve this ideal; more precisely, it shows you how to speak 'dog' so that you can communicate effectively with your four-legged friend.

How to use this book

You will be amazed at how much you can achieve in just two days of training your dog to respond to your directions and behave as you want, so long as you go about it correctly. Then, over the following weeks, you can reinforce everything your dog has learned, until you achieve your training goals.

Bear in mind, however, that trying to do everything at once rarely works effectively, particularly when there is more than one area or problem to deal with. If you use the advice given here as a series of stepping stones, you will find that the level of training for which you are aiming

HE OR SHE?

Throughout this book, we have referred to dogs as 'he', but unless otherwise stated, the advice given is equally applicable to female dogs.

comes more easily to both you and your dog.

There are no set time limits to how long it should take to fully train a dog – and, in fact, setting time limits can be counter-productive if the owner thinks his dog is not progressing as it should. The length of time it takes to achieve success very much depends on the individual aptitude of both owner and dog.

Established behaviour traits such as aggression, barking, chasing other animals and car travel problems usually take time and effort on your part. Continual training and reinforcement of lessons are the key to success. But you can make a very good start in one weekend – and may be surprised at just how much your dog improves.

How long should training sessions last?

This depends on a number of things:

• The age of your dog
• Type/breed (some have more aptitude for learning than others)
• Your dog's fitness and health

Puppies do not have a prolonged attention span. Three ten-minute sessions a day teaching, say, collar and leash training, are better than one 30-minute session. This is because the chances of you finishing the session on a positive note are greater than if you were to carry on longer.

Training periods are also dictated by the results you get: if you have, for example, allowed ten minutes to teach your dog how to sit on command and he does it in two, then finish there on that positive note. The dog will remember this and be more receptive to pick up where you left off at the next training session.

There are few things more relaxing and restorative than returning home from a hard day's work and receiving an ecstatic welcome, then taking your dog out to play to relieve your mental strain and physical aches. If only our relationships with other people were so simple!

TRAINER'S TIP

10–15 minutes of concentrated training in a one-hour period is the maximum most dogs can cope with mentally and physically. Although dog training classes run for one hour or so, there are usually about six dogs involved, meaning that the trainer devotes ten minutes of one-to-one with each dog.

Why you need a well-trained pet

An untrained dog can be a real nuisance – a hazard to himself, his owner, and other people and animals. Owning an undisciplined pet can result in:

• Visitors no longer wanting to call for fear of being jumped on and covered with hair and slobber.
• Injury to you at home or on walks due to your dog barging into you, pulling you along or being aggressive.

• Injury to someone else caused by your dog ignoring your recall commands and attacking or chasing them, or by the unleashed dog running into the street and causing a traffic accident.
• Your dog being hurt or killed by a car.
• Legal action against you for damage caused by your dog.
• Damage to your home.
• Stress for all concerned: for you as well as your dog.

Read and digest

Read this book through and you will see what order training should comprise. In addition you will learn how to understand and correctly relate to your dog – which is essential if you are to train him effectively – and how to apply the principles of no-fuss, common-sense training.

If you can only commit yourself to, say, two 15-minute sessions in one weekend with no continual training in between, but still expect your pet to be well-behaved and punish him when he does something unacceptable to you, the question you must ask yourself is 'should I have a dog?'

Mark your progress

Keep a diary of your dog's training progress: write down what areas need improving, then how long the training session lasted and how he responded to your teaching methods. Note both positive and negative aspects. Not only will this prove an invaluable reference for you, it will also help a dog trainer and/or canine behaviourist assess you both should you enlist their help – particularly where behavioural problems are concerned.

Keep it fun

The key point to remember when training, whether it is for five minutes or 15, is to keep it fun. This way the dog is more likely to remain focused on, and therefore responsive to, you. And you'll both enjoy yourselves, which, after all, is the whole point of having a dog!

Man's best friend

A dog is the ultimate companion. He won't judge our sins (real or imagined), get angry with us, lie

Having some idea of how a dog thinks and feels goes a very long way towards achieving success in training him, and the more that you learn about the subject, the more you will accomplish.

to us or cheat us. He may become miserable if we treat him badly, but he will never blame us. A dog's innocence and trust in us are complete.

It is well-known that dogs are great stress relievers. They are often more receptive to your emotions than fellow humans. They will happily listen to your daily moans and groans, celebrate with you, and comfort you in your hour of need.

However, things are not quite so rosy if you have a dog who nearly knocks you over when he greets you, won't let you sit on your favourite chair, repeatedly soils in the house, is aggressive towards people and other animals, chews anything he can get his teeth on and ignores the commands you give. That's when having a dog is simply anything but fun!

Handling and training your dog correctly from puppyhood helps to stop behavioural problems developing, and retraining an adult dog can often correct those that already exist. The knack is in knowing just how to go about it, and this book will give you training methods that are easy to understand and implement. You don't need fancy gadgets, expensive equipment or a degree in dog psychology – just some common sense, a willingness to understand how your dog's mind works, and the desire to turn him into a wonderful companion that everyone will love. Your dog deserves it!

Are you ready to become a dog owner?

The question you must ask yourself is: 'I want a dog, but would a dog want me as his owner?' Successful relationships are based on positive two-way communication and respect, and you will find that understanding how your dog thinks helps you to establish a more mutually rewarding partnership with him.

In this book you will learn how to become a fair and positive leader to your dog and how to be clear, consistent and respectful in your actions and directions towards him. Then you will be able to define a code of practice and behaviour that your dog understands and will respond to in the way that you wish him to.

Essential equipment
Buying suitable equipment from the start helps to make caring for and training your dog easier, and this topic is covered in detail on pages 30–33 to help you avoid expensive mistakes. For example, you'd be surprised at what a difference it makes if you have a leash that is the correct length for the size of your dog!

Puppy training
By following the clear instructions that are provided on pages 34–53, you will discover how to guide and train your new puppy so that he develops into a well-mannered adult of whom you can be justly proud.

TRAINER'S TIP

Where dogs are concerned, the pack instinct prevails. With this in mind, you must ensure that *you*, and not your dog, are the leader of your particular 'pack'.

This section also demonstrates that there are many aspects to dog ownership, some of which you may never previously have thought about. Prospective owners must consider all of them carefully before taking the plunge and acquiring a dog, for both their own and the animal's sake.

Obedience training
Successful training is based on the simple principle of reward. Generally, dogs love to please their owners, and they enjoy doing so even more when they are rewarded for it. Reward-based training is, therefore, the key to having a happy and obedient dog. Food is an all-important aspect of canine life, so using food rewards is likely to achieve the training results you require. Using reward training in a variety of situations is explained in detail on pages 54–85.

Corrective training
Knowing why dogs 'misbehave' will enable you to find solutions to specific problems. The case histories on pages 86–125 illustrate just how effectively the methods described in this and other sections of the book work in practice.

Food training–teaching your dog to sit, stay, and wait before he is given his food and then to wait for permission to eat–is a good start in achieving obedience in all other areas. Learn how to food train correctly and then how to use this principle as a fast and effective route to a well-behaved dog.

Taking on a rescue dog

Many people like the idea of providing a rescue dog with a home (see pages 28–29), but the reality of living with one can be very different from what you imagined. Behavioural problems can and often do arise when the owner is ill-prepared for a dog whose past experiences and behaviour are unknown. However, when you get it right, the rewards for both owner and pet can be great.

1 Be the perfect owner

So you have always wanted a dog. Well, it is easy enough to go out and get one; the hard part is caring for him correctly.

If you have never owned a dog before, you will find that it isn't as simple as you may imagine. There is more to looking after your pet than giving him a bowl of food once a day, taking him for a walk around the block and spending ten minutes or so throwing a ball for him to chase and retrieve. Even if you have experience with dogs (perhaps your family had one when you were a child) the reality of having your own dog can be quite a shock when you discover exactly what is involved in caring for him.

You may also be disappointed if you acquire a replacement for a much-loved doggy pal who has passed away, only to discover that the new arrival's behaviour is nothing like that of his obedient and good-natured predecessor.

An ideal owner is one who trains their pet to be a 'good citizen'; obedient, good-natured, and a pleasure to own.

A dog is for life

By now it should be clear that dogs are not simply consumable items that you can bring home to fit neatly into your life and provide you with comfort and entertainment, with no inconvenience whatsoever to you. Dog ownership is richly rewarding if you do it right but thoroughly miserable for all concerned if you don't.

Before you set out to find a four-legged friend to share your life, there are some important things you must consider to ensure that you will be the owner every dog deserves.

Choose the right dog

You should choose a breed and type of dog based on the environment you can offer it. There are several important factors to take into account.

Your lifestyle • Some dogs dislike being left 'home alone' while their owners are at work and will suffer separation anxiety. This can lead to behavioural problems, such as house soiling, barking and chewing.

Your home • Ideally, you should live in a house large enough to accommodate your family and your chosen size and type of dog, with plenty of space for everyone. If you do not have a garden that is large enough for exercising your dog

Along with feeding, handling, and training your pet correctly, make sure you set aside plenty of time every day for the most important activity: having some fun together.

adequately, you must be able to provide him with two walks per day of around one hour each. This should ideally include some playtime in an area where he can be safely off-leash.

If you are house-proud, you must be prepared for a lot of extra work to keep your home sweet-smelling and free of dog hair and muddy paw prints. For minimal mess – and stress for all concerned – do not choose a large, hairy, slobbery type of dog.

Can you afford a dog?

The average dog lives for around 12 years, which is a long time to commit mentally, physically and financially to another being. Apart from the initial expense of buying your dog, neutering, and the essential equipment you will need, regular financial outlays include:

- Food

- Routine vaccinations

- Veterinary check-ups

- Internal and external parasite treatments

- Holiday boarding fees

- Health and third party/public liability insurance

- Training classes

- Replacement equipment as necessary

- Specialized grooming care for certain coats

Your temperament • Since dogs can sense human emotions, a stressed owner is likely to end up with a stressed pet. Dogs respond best to calm, consistent handling. Shouting at or hitting your pet will confuse and frighten him, resulting in behavioural problems. You need to be patient and controlled enough not to become angry if your dog does something that is perceived as wrong.

Time • Are you sure you have enough spare time to exercise, train and play with a dog? If you get a puppy, during the first couple of months you will need to spend a lot of time house training and establishing basic obedience. Later, you will need to allow at least two hours every day for care and exercise. Dog training classes – preferably weekly, but at least once a month – will help keep you both on the right track.

Key points

An ideal dog owner is:

- Consistent and clear with directions
- Patient
- Self-controlled
- Calm
- Fair
- Positive
- Understanding

A dog is a living being who possesses feelings, a mind of his own and a 'language' that you must learn to understand in order to communicate with him effectively.

INSURANCE

Not taking out suitable insurance cover can prove a false economy. It could mean being faced with a massive veterinary bill if your dog needs extensive treatment, while a lawsuit against you for personal or property damage caused by your dog could leave you facing financial ruin. Shop around for the best insurance deal and ask your vet for recommendations, then remember to read the small print on policy proposals.

If there are children or young adults in the household, you must teach them to respect the dog and to handle and speak to him correctly. It is advisable to steer clear of the more naturally dominant breeds and choose one of the more gentle, equable types.

Case history: Choose your companion carefully

Just like humans, dogs are individuals, each with his own unique personality and behaviour traits. To some extent, however, you can predict how certain breeds will perform and fit into your lifestyle – or not. The following story, which involves a traditionally bred outdoor hunting dog is a prime example.

The dog • Two-year-old Jack Russell Penny was 'a wonderful little lady who is good with children and all other animals – and a great ratter'. So said Penny's tearful owner, who was moving abroad and couldn't take the dog with her, to prospective new owner Karen. Once settled into her new home, it turned out that Penny was all of these things, but she was *not* a good house dog.

The problem • Penny urinated and defecated in the house; in fact, she made a point of quite happily spending all day outside, coming in only to eat her meals, soil the carpet and chew the furniture. Despite all efforts within her capabilities, Karen (a full-time working mother) could not cope. She simply hadn't the time or money to retrain this little outdoor dog into being an indoor pet.

The solution • Karen looked for a suitable new home for Penny, and finally succeeded when Jennifer answered her advertisement for 'problem Jack Russell free to good home'. Jennifer loved dogs. She was at home all day, wasn't house-proud, and could devote the time and energy necessary to care for and re-train a less-than-perfect pet successfully.

This is a good example of how two different owners were perfect in their own way. One had the courage to admit she couldn't cope and strove to find a solution, while the other was willing to offer Penny a home and solve the problem, no matter what.

2 Understand your dog

Dogs evolved as pack animals and this instinct is still strong today. If you learn to understand canine instinct, how dogs 'talk' to each other and what their body language means, you will be better able to communicate with your dog.

Survival of the fittest

In any social group of animals, there has to be a pecking order, or chaos will ensue. In a canine pack, the dog who is mentally and physically strongest asserts himself as the leader, with the rest accepting their lesser roles and relying on the 'boss' to provide for and protect them. Animal nature being what it is, however, there is always an element of competition for the prime position.

The instinct for self-preservation is strong. From day one, puppies strive for the best position at feeding time, with siblings pushing and shoving each other in their attempts to latch on to the nipples that produce the most milk. The strongest thrive; the weakest are lucky to survive.

At weaning, the most forceful pup gets the lion's share of any food mum brings back, but he has to eat quickly before the other pups gang up on him and steal his dinner. The pups also learn social skills from their peers, including how to socialize, behave, hunt, play and fight. How well they learn these skills determines how well they integrate into the pack. As adults, the fastest, fittest, strongest and most cunning dogs are better equipped to find food as well as to guard their territory against intruders.

All of these instincts and characteristics are strong in domesticated dogs. A puppy's upbringing determines his character, so the better he is socialized with humans and accustomed to household living as a youngster, the better he will be able to deal with his future role as a canine companion to his human 'pack'.

If you take the time and trouble to understand how your dog's natural instincts affect his behaviour and apply that knowledge to your training, you will help to lay the foundation for a mutually rewarding relationship.

CHILD SAFETY

Never leave young children alone with a dog, no matter how good-natured or trustworthy you think the animal is. Often quite unintentionally, children can harass a dog unmercifully, until he can take no more and bites to warn them off (as he would an unruly pup in the pack). This is unacceptable in a human environment, so for everyone's sake, do not put the dog or children in a situation in which they are at risk.

Dogs are naturally sociable, but for an equable pack environment, an appropriate hierarchy needs to be established. The dog on the right is warning the other two not to enter his space, and they are deferring to his superiority.

Pack pluses

Living in a pack has many advantages. Hunting as a group means that:

• Food is easier to find and take.
• There is comfort, safety and security in numbers.
• There are plenty of opportunities for play (for pure pleasure) and mock-fighting (practice for the real thing).
• There are many potential partners around to ensure perpetuation of the species.

Key points ☑

• Understand and work with your dog's natural instincts.

• Make him aware from day one that it is you that is the pack leader.

• Do not put the dog in situations in which his instincts may make him lash out and bite.

• Avoid anthropomorphism.

Anthropomorphism

Many owners are unintentionally guilty of attributing human characteristics to their animals, to everyone's detriment. Examples of this include:

Attributing guilt

An owner may find that her dog has soiled in the house and say that the dog looked guilty because he knew he had done wrong. To a dog, however, defecating is just a natural function, and he has nothing about which to feel 'guilty'.

To uninformed humans, the dog's expression and body language may indicate that he knows he has done something wrong, when in fact he is displaying fear and/or submission, having sensed his owner's displeasure. However, he does not necessarily associate that displeasure with having made a mess on the floor!

Overfeeding

An owner may overfeed a dog or give him treats between meals because 'he looks hungry'. Instinctively, dogs are food-motivated (in the wild, they never know when their next meal will be), but if adequately fed, they are not hungry. If you fall victim to those 'pleading' eyes, all you will do is allow your dog to train you in the art of room service, make him obese and thereby shorten his life.

3 Body language

You can gauge the mental state of a dog from his posture and his facial and vocal expressions. As you get used to your own pet, you will learn his individual and unique ways of communicating.

   Generally, a stiff stance with jerky movements indicates aggression, uncertainty and fear, while a relaxed posture and smooth movements mean the dog is at ease. A wagging tail does not always indicate a happy, friendly dog. You have to take into account the rest of his body language before deciding whether he is a friend or a foe. Look beyond the wagging tail and note the dog's hackles (the top of his shoulder, just behind his neck), his body stance and his facial expressions.

calm and alert
The pricked ears and kind, interested expression indicate a **calm, content and inquisitive** dog. This breed, the German Shepherd, was developed in its native country to herd sheep, so its natural instincts are to guard and be watchful, and the expression here shows the breed at its best – alert, generous and intelligent.

Reading your dog's body language

Wagging a raised, stiff tail	Implies tension and potential aggression
Wagging a low tail, possibly between his legs	Indicates fear and/or submission
Energetically wagging a tail at half-mast	Usually a good sign, generally meaning the dog is neither tense nor depressed
Wagging a tail with a relaxed body stance, 'smiley' face and lolling ears	The dog is looking to play or get kind attention
Hackles raised (hair standing up and bushed out), legs stiff and eyes fixed	Indicates a dog on his guard and ready to attack if necessary

These two pictures show happy dogs with totally different personalities.

The young German Shepherd (above) is energetic, curious, and always ready to play and investigate, while the cross-breed (below) is much older, with a more laid-back and quiet personality, and is not as energetic.

intense and watchful

This expression – the so-called Collie eye – illustrates perfectly an **intense and watchful** dog, but not necessarily an aggressive one. A herding type, the Border Collie was bred to manage sheep and the instinct to herd (be it sheep, other animals or people) is deeply ingrained. Such dogs are extremely intense in their emotional make-up and need careful and sympathetic handling to bring out the best in them. If you get it right, they make fantastic companions; if you get it wrong, the dog will display all manner of behavioural 'aberrations', and both dog and owner will be frustrated and miserable.

frightened

This is a **frightened** dog. It is a pitiful sight, and one no owner should be proud to see. The stance indicates a browbeaten dog whose upbringing has been less than ideal. If a dog commonly displays this posture, he will need a great deal of confidence building in order to make him more emotionally stable and able to enjoy life.

Each displays a relaxed body stance and happy, kind, facial expression in his own unique way. These examples demonstrate that knowing your own dog's personality is the key to being able to interpret his emotional state at any given moment.

Key points

- Learn how to interpret your dog's body language, and thus recognize his state of mind.

- Tail-wagging does not necessarily mean that a dog is friendly.

- A tense body indicates uncertainty, fear or potential aggression, while a soft body stance and fluid movements mean a dog is relaxed and happy.

- A dog's natural instincts dictate his behaviour, so you must take that into account as you work with your pet.

- Find out about different breeds' inherent traits and use this knowledge to choose your ideal dog.

unhappy or ill
This body posture indicates a **depressed and unhappy** dog. Such a stance could be due to a stressful atmosphere (a disruptive household, or physical/mental abuse) or because he is experiencing physical discomfort due to illness.

warning/submission
A classic example of **warning off** and **submission**. The dog on the right is displaying a 'don't mess with me or I'll attack' stance, while the dog on the left is adopting an 'OK, I'm backing off and won't bother you again' pose.

Some dogs are more stoical than others and will put up with considerable discomfort before their owners realize something is wrong. Despite a raging toothache, for example, some dogs do not whine or appear unwell, and it is only when the owner notices that the dog takes longer to eat or is not eating at all that a problem becomes apparent.

This is why it is essential to check your dog thoroughly every day for any unusual lumps or sore spots. Check his eyes, ears and mouth for foreign bodies or any sign of inflammation, and watch for irregularities in behaviour, eating and defecating.

aggression
In **squaring-up**, the dog on the left is displaying the attitude of being 'armed to attack': his hackles are raised, his teeth are bared and his body stance is tense, ready to propel him into defence against an apparently hostile approach from another. Yet dogs will attack with intent only if they deem it vital for their own well-being: in the wild, harming another pack member is always a last resort, because an incapacitated dog means that there is one fewer member available to guard and find food for the group as a whole.

submission
A **submissive** dog adopts this body posture. Crouching and licking his lips or yawning indicates 'I'm insignificant, so please don't harm me!'

4 Why does he do that?

Dogs display a number of traits that humans find strange or even disgusting (eating faeces is a prime example). Yet dogs do what they do for a reason. As far as they are concerned, they are doing nothing wrong, and they become confused when we scold them.

Knowing why dogs do certain things will enable you to cope better with them as they occur. Do not to get cross with your dog; instead, prevent him doing potentially harmful things by distracting him with a game or toy or by avoiding difficult situations.

Natural behaviour
The following pictures show examples of the natural behaviour your dog is likely to display at some time in his life, with an explanation of why he exhibits such behaviour, and advice on what to do about it.

grass eating
Eating grass aids your dog's digestion. When we get indigestion, we take an antacid; when dogs feel nauseated, they eat grass to induce vomiting and rid their stomachs of whatever ails them. Excessive grass-eating should be investigated by a vet.

drinking dirty water
Some dogs seem to love **drinking from dirty puddles** or even slime-covered ponds, much to their owners' horror. It is wise not to let your dog do this, because the water could be polluted with chemicals or harbour parasites. And take care when preparing your car for winter. Dogs seem to find spilled antifreeze irresistible, but it is a deadly poison for them.

it's mine!
Guarding food or a toy, by growling or snapping at anyone who approaches to take it away, is a dog's way of saying 'this is mine and you cannot have it'. This line of defence is inappropriate in a human environment, and you must teach your dog from an early age to relinquish items without a fuss.

scent communication
Sniffing the ground and other dogs' backsides and faces is a very important part of canine communication. By sniffing the ground, dogs can identify territorial boundaries and mating possibilities, while sniffing another dog's rear end identifies its sex and whether it is a potential friend or foe. Dogs sniff at human crotches for the same reasons.

'scooting'
When a dog scrapes his bottom along the ground, propelling himself forwards with his forelegs, this **'scooting'** action indicates that he is having discomfort in his anal area. This could be due to worms, blocked anal glands, constipation or soreness. Such behaviour requires veterinary attention to determine the cause and provide a solution.

possession

Instinct dictates that to let another take away food will result in hunger. This principle of **possession** extends to toys and other items that a dog has: to give them up is a sign of weakness. In pet dogs, not letting go of something must be discouraged from an early age, otherwise aggression problems may develop. It is fine to let a non-aggressive or non-possessive dog occasionally win the toy in a tug game to keep his play motivation high, but make sure this is the exception rather than the rule.

eating faeces

Eating and rolling in other animals' faeces is a habit most owners find repulsive. To a dog, however, eating faeces provides essential nutrients that his own body is lacking, while rolling in them (and also on dead animals) is a way of masking his own scent in preparation for hunting.

it's down there somewhere...

Digging indicates that the dog is looking for food or for quarry to chase, catch and eat. Hunting dogs and terriers are particularly prone to digging in areas that their sense of smell tells them will be rewarding, so unless you want your garden rearranged, reserve a special area in which your dog can indulge in this harmless habit. If you bury a toy or bone in this special spot, your dog will get a reward for his efforts and keep returning to it to try his luck again.

Other traits

grass-scratching

Scratching up grass with the front and back legs after urinating and defecating is a way of marking territory: odours left by the scent glands in the dog's feet, along with the visual sign of disturbed earth, alert other animals to his presence in that area. Another possibility is that such scratching indicates that the dog is displaying relief at having finished emptying his bladder or bowels. There is an air of satisfied finality about this action, perhaps indicating that the dog no longer feels vulnerable to attack while relieving himself.

pursuit

Chasing another animal in the wild is the first step in finding food or warning off intruders, so dogs find the experience very enjoyable and rewarding.

Marking territory

Urinating against trees and defecating on or next to another dog's droppings is a highly effective 'messaging service'. The scent left behind tells other dogs who has passed that way, their sex and their size (the reason some male dogs leave their excretions as high as possible).

Howling

This is the vocal signal that wild dogs use to call the pack together, which is why dogs left alone in a house may howl. It is their way of trying to make absent owners return to the fold. Being very social creatures, most dogs feel insecure and unhappy when they are alone.

5 Respect your dog

In the same way that humans can, dogs can sometimes become stressed by the hectic pace of modern life. Maybe they don't go out to work like their owners, but they do have to put up with those owners rushing around frantically in the morning and sometimes coming home tired and irritable at night.

Just as you respect human family members' feelings, you must consider how your behaviour affects your dog. Whatever your emotional state, put that of your dog first; don't let your actions or tone of voice convey impatience. Being unselfish about fulfilling his mental and physical needs is the first step in respecting your pet.

Rules of respect for a dog

Approach • Avoid sudden movements or loud noises directed at your dog, which he could construe as aggressive.

Reward • Dogs love to please, so always reward him for good behaviour.

Food and drink • Always feed your dog a suitable diet in the correct daily quantity for his size and energy requirements. Be sure he has a constant supply of fresh, clean water to drink.

Attention and exercise • Give your dog plenty of daily affection and playtime, sufficient exercise off-leash and social interaction with his own kind.

Health care • Have your dog vaccinated against common diseases and treated as necessary for parasites such as fleas and ticks. Take him for veterinary attention whenever you think he may be ill.

Understanding • Do not reprimand your dog for displaying natural behaviours such as rolling in or eating other animals' droppings or sniffing under other dogs' tails. Simply distract him with a food treat or a toy.

Possessions • Provide your dog with toys to play with so he will be less likely to take or chew other items in the house.

Companionship • Being social creatures, most dogs thrive in the company of humans. To deny them companionship for long periods is unfair and can lead to problem behaviour.

Elimination • Provide your dog with an area where he knows he can relieve himself, and always clean up after him.

Safety • Do not put your dog in situations that are hazardous or make him uncomfortable. Do not take him to places where there will be large crowds of people, for example, or where there may be uncontrolled, potentially aggressive dogs. Never leave him unattended in a car on a warm day, where heatstroke and suffocation are real risks.

TRAINER'S TIP

• Canine hearing is much more acute than that of humans. Loud noises, therefore, cause dogs discomfort and fear. Do not raise your voice in anger towards your dog or subject him to blaring music or loud volume from the television.

• Avoid prolonged eye contact with dogs; they perceive it as a threat.

• Make sure that everyone in the family sticks by the training rules. For example, if one person does not allow the dog on the furniture, another should not encourage him to jump on the sofa.

• Do not allow games to become rough or encourage the dog to play-bite or jump all over you. Such games tend to get out of hand, someone gets hurt, and the dog cannot understand why he is scolded for something he has just been encouraged to do.

Key points

- Provide your dog with a place of his own where he can relax without being disturbed.

- Stick to the training rules.

- Do not raise your voice in anger.

- Do not use physical violence.

- Fulfil your dog's mental and physical needs.

When petting your dog, be sure that you give him attention in a non-threatening way. The kind of petting shown below is only possible once you have built up a solid, trusting relationship with an even-tempered and placid dog.

Giving him space

Dogs are quick to sense their owners' emotions, and when all is not well, they can be upset.

Thus your dog needs his own private space to retreat to and feel secure, until he senses that you are in a good mood and ready to give him attention.

It can also be a place to hide away from the children when he has had enough of play, to relax and to sleep without being disturbed.

6 Command and reward

When training your dog, remember that he will learn to associate a word with an action, so you must be very aware of what your body as well as your voice is telling him. For example, if you are verbally trying to encourage the dog to come to you, make your body language as welcoming as your tone of voice.

Rewarding your dog every time he acts as you wish on a particular word-action command will lead to a learned response. Eventually, that response will become automatic every time you say the command and display the action, similar to the way you would automatically check your wrist if someone asked you the time.

Sit
One of the most useful commands to teach your dog is **'sit'**. See pages 62–63.

Down
The **'down'** command is a natural progression from sit. See pages 64–65.

Most dogs will do anything for a tasty treat. Once you identify your pet's favourites, you'll have a great training tool. Interestingly, some dogs adore fresh fruit and vegetables such as apples, green vegetables and tender young carrots, while almost every dog is partial to hot dogs and cooked liver. Some commercial treats are also very popular.

Keep some desirable toys aside so they have increased value as special rewards. When training, give your dog his favourite 'high-value' toy for performing a required action, let him play with it for a few minutes, then take it away so that it does not become ordinary.

If you use treats to reward your dog while training, be sure you have a supply in your pocket or a bumbag and that they are chopped up into tiny pieces, otherwise your dog will get very fat very quickly.

'Rewarding' inappropriate behaviour

Beware of unconsciously rewarding undesirable behaviour, or your dog will assume that his inappropriate actions are acceptable. For example, do not let him push through a door in front of you, but make him wait. If you let him through unchecked, the fact that he has gone out just as he wanted is a reward in itself.

Stay
Sometimes a dog is uncomfortable with the '**stay**' command, but, if taught correctly, he'll soon be happy to obey. See pages 66–67.

Here
Having your dog come to you when you command '**here**' is invaluable. See pages 76–77.

Good boy
Until your dog displays a learned response, you should reward each desired response to your commands. Thereafter, reward at random to keep his response levels high.

Use 'train brain'

• Be consistent in your commands and actions. Use the same words for commands, such as 'down', 'sit', 'stay', 'fetch' and 'give'.

• Changing commands will confuse your dog. Be consistent, even if it takes a while for your dog to learn them. Make sure that other family members use the same commands and actions and follow the same code of behaviour for your dog.

• Reward desired behaviour and your dog will learn more quickly.

• Verbal commands should be encouraging and given at an even pitch.

• Keep commands clear and well spaced (at least at first) so you do not confuse your dog.

• If your dog has learned to ignore a command and probably thinks it means something else (such as you saying 'heel' when he is walking ahead of you and pulling, so that he associates 'heel' with pulling) then use a different word when you begin re-training (in this case 'side').

• Never raise your voice in anger; it is counterproductive.

Commercial training aids

Training aids such as clickers, training discs, whistles, and remote or sound-activated liquid spray (not electric shock!) collars can be very effective in certain circumstances. But before using any of them, ask a trainer who is skilled in their use to show you how to apply them correctly and effectively. Otherwise, you may end up confusing and/or frightening your pet.

7 Rescue dogs

A dog in a rescue centre is there for a reason: someone couldn't cope with his behaviour. He may be aggressive, destructive, not toilet trained, or even all three. What makes you think you can cope with him when his previous owners couldn't?

When taking on a rescue dog, you must be willing to give the animal as long as he needs to settle into his new home. Do not expect a miraculous change in his behaviour just because you are now his owner. Be prepared for anything up to a year (or more) of remedial work. Some dogs recover quickly from the traumas of their past experiences and adapt well to a new home, but many do not.

The right reasons

Many dog trainers have had people come to them complaining that the rescue dog they have acquired is 'misbehaving'. It often turns out that they adopted the dog because they 'felt sorry for him' or 'he looked cute' or they were 'passing' and once they had gone in they 'just couldn't come out without one'.

Dogs who have been abandoned or mistreated need time to recover from the treatment they have received and the way of life they have had to follow in order to survive.

Key points

- Remember that the kennel staff will be able to give you only limited information about dogs in their care.

- Be aware that many of the dog's behaviour traits and his temperament will become apparent only after you get him home.

- Ask yourself if you are willing to invest time and money in training and remedial work, possibly for a prolonged period.

- Note that it is a good idea to discuss re-homing a rescue dog with a couple of trainers first.

- Think very carefully before committing yourself.

These are not the correct reasons for taking on a rescue dog, for either you or the animal. The bottom line is that no matter what the dog looks like and no matter how sorry you feel for him, you and your family have to be able to live comfortably with him in your home.

Although it is tempting to take the whole family with you to choose a dog, don't. Leave the children at home, as their pleading may persuade you to choose a dog that is totally unsuitable. Once you have seen a potential pet, ask the kennel staff about him and satisfy yourself that he will be right for you and you for him. Only then should you take the kids to meet him and see how they react to each other.

Case history: rehabilitation

With correct training, it is perfectly possible to rehabilitate a 'lost cause', as is illustrated by this account of a confirmed vehicle chaser.

The dog • Part-bred Border Collie Bruno was a rescue centre resident. A confirmed vehicle chaser, he had been there for about nine months, and at three years old it was thought his behaviour would never change.

The problem • Bruno had a wonderful temperament and adored people. Several prospective owners had taken a real shine to him, but were put off because as soon as he left the centre and got anywhere near the road, he reverted to pulling on the leash and trying to attack cars as they passed.

The solution • Keith Davis was asked to do some remedial work with Bruno so that he could find a home. First Keith took him out into an enclosed exercise area to assess his general behaviour and found that Bruno was a typical Border Collie type: full of life and keen to play.

When Bruno was fitted with a headcollar and half-check collar (see pages 40–41 and 60–61), with the leash clipped to both collars, there was an immediate improvement. Over the next three days Keith spent an hour a day with Bruno at a set of traffic lights. First, he sat on a low wall, using favourite treats to keep Bruno's attention on him as traffic went by. Then, as the cars stopped at the lights, Keith walked Bruno up and down the road, then sat down again. After this, Keith gave a treat only when the dog was focused on him while traffic passed. Bruno soon got the idea: chasing after traffic went unrewarded; not chasing traffic got him a treat!

By the third day, Bruno was content to sit and watch the traffic go by without leaping at it. At the same time, using the correct equipment on him had resolved the pulling problem, and he was re-homed soon afterwards. To date, his problems have not recurred.

8 Essential equipment

You will need to purchase a number of items of equipment in order to make life comfortable for both you and your dog.

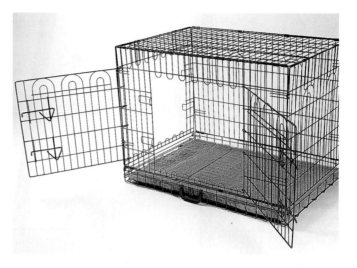

Also called a den or cage, a **crate** serves as a bed and is useful for toilet training, for keeping the dog separate from the family when necessary and for safety when travelling with your dog.

Choose a **bed** that will be big enough for the dog when he is fully grown, made from a washable material and with raised sides to protect against draughts. **Bedding** should be thick enough for the dog to lie on comfortably, and made from washable, quick-drying fabric.

Stainless steel or glazed ceramic **food and water bowls** are the most hygienic.

Buy a selection of durable **toys** for your dog, keeping some aside for use as special rewards.

Ask a trainer's advice on the most suitable **collar and leash** for your type of dog.

1 Fixed length cord leash – not the preferred choice of most dog trainers as it cannot be extended or retracted as necessary.

2 Three-in-one medium-weight training leash – good for basic and intermediate training. It gives close control and allows the start of distance work, for example recall and stay.

3 Long training line – training lines are available in different lengths to suit your requirements, and used for extended recall and stay exercises, and for tracking exercises. Good for allowing a dog freedom whilst retaining control, for example when there is livestock in the vicinity.

4 Three-quarter chain collar with adjustable leather strap – suitable for fully trained dogs. Not suitable for training as it does not have enough flexibility.

5 Half-check fabric collar with clip fastener – suitable for basic and subsequent training due to its flexibility and 'kindness'.

Boredom-beater

A filled Kong toy will help keep your dog occupied when you are not there, or you can use it to distract him when necessary.

1 Fill the Kong with unsalted cream cheese, and push biscuit treats down into it.

2 Seal in the cheese by smoothing it down with a knife. Give the toy to your dog to enjoy!

GROOMING GEAR

You will need some grooming equipment to keep your dog's coat and skin in good condition. Your dog's breeder can advise you about the best tools for the job, or contact a local grooming parlour.

FIRST AID KIT

It is a good idea to have one on hand. Choose a kit that contains the following basic items:

- ✓ Saline solution
- ✓ Small bowl
- ✓ Small curved and blunt-tipped scissors
- ✓ Antiseptic cream
- ✓ Wipes
- ✓ Cold pack
- ✓ Self-sticking bandage
- ✓ Gauze swabs
- ✓ Cotton wool
- ✓ Surgical tape
- ✓ Tweezers

Activity toys and chews will keep your dog occupied. Chews must be given only under supervision in case of choking.

1 Durable rubber toy – designed for play and filling with treats.

2 As above – but this design makes it even trickier to get the treats out.

3 Kong activity toy – almost indestructible, so suitable for dogs with powerful jaws.

4 Cereal biscuit bones – these come in different sizes to suit all dogs.

5 & 7 Meat-flavoured soft chews – most dogs will do anything for these tasty treats.

6 Roasted pig ear – a great chew treat that will also help clean your dog's teeth.

8 Tough plastic meat-impregnated chew – great for teething dogs.

9 Rawhide chew – these come in different thicknesses and help keep teeth clean.

Having your dog loose in the car is a hazard to the driver, the passengers and the dog. When travelling with your dog, make sure that he is safely secured by a **harness, crate or dog grille**.

A **stair gate** is useful for keeping your dog out of certain areas of the house, but since it allows him to see his family he won't feel isolated.

Case history: the right equipment

The dog • Troy was a boisterous 18-month-old German Pointer. Sharon and Peter had every intention of taking him to training classes from the start, but they had put it off for various reasons.

The problem • Sharon found that she couldn't handle Troy on walks; Peter was strong, but even he struggled to hold the dog.

The solution • On assessing Troy at training class, Keith Davis saw that his collar and leash were made of heavy chain. Such weight is uncomfortable for a dog, and half the problem may have been that Troy was jumping about to try to relieve the pressure on his neck.

Keith fitted him with a headcollar, plus a half-check collar for additional safety. Within ten minutes, Troy was walking on the leash better than ever before. Sharon and Peter were asked to work on certain exercises and return to class the following week.

When they returned, Troy was back in his chain collar. The couple said that while Sharon used the headcollar, Peter didn't. Troy had again become uncontrollable. Keith told both of them to use the headcollar and half-check when walking Troy. With correct use of the prescribed equipment, Troy progressed rapidly over the weeks and became a pleasure to take for walks.

WEEKEND PUPPY TRAINING:
the first 7 steps

Training plan

Weekend 1:
- Teach puppy to recognize and answer to its name.
- Begin socializing: accustom puppy to household sights and sounds – television, washing machine, vacuum cleaner, etc.
- Begin food training by handling the puppy while it is eating.
- Start toilet and crate training.

Weekend 2:
- Commence collar and leash training.
- Have puppy meet other people of all ages and sexes. Remember to praise and reward where appropriate, not to scold – simply ignore pup if he displays inappropriate behaviour.
- Begin any behavioural training as necessary, such as for play biting and/ or jumping up.

Weekend 3:
- Get puppy used to seeing and being near other animals, such as companion pets, as well as larger animals where possible such as cattle. For safety ensure he is not allowed to chase these animals.

Weekend 4:
- Introduce car travel.
- Once he's been vaccinated, start accustoming puppy to sights and sounds on walks – keep these short and close to home at first.

Weekend 5:
- Gradually extend car journeys.
- Start going to puppy training classes once he has been vaccinated.
- By now puppy will be going to his crate for time out or to rest in 'his' den. You can either leave the crate where it is, or replace it with a bed.

Congratulations – you have a puppy! All you need to do is train him to be the ideal companion. The first weeks of his life, while he was in the litter, set the foundations. Now, correct training will set the standard of behaviour you can come to expect as your youngster matures. How good his manners will ultimately be depends on how well you teach him the social rules of living in a human environment. And you can start to set him on the right path in just a weekend!

Puppies and young dogs need plenty of rest, just like babies and young children.

TRAINER'S TIP

In the early months, avoid over-exercising your puppy, as this can cause serious damage to his growing bones and developing muscles, tendons and ligaments.

Once your cute little bundle of fluff is safely home and settled in, he will probably start getting you to run around after him – but only if you let him. While you need to be gentle and sympathetic towards your puppy, you also need to be quite strict; otherwise, you will soon find yourself exhausted by his needs and demands.

What you need to teach your puppy

In order to grow into amenable, house-trained, obedient and well-mannered adults, puppies need to be taught how to be all of these things.

The Training plan chart opposite provides an example of the steps to take to start training. Detailed instructions about how to train puppies can be found in the following pages .

Remember to keep training sessions short – puppies have a limited attention span and get tired quickly. End sessions on a positive note, even if it means going back a step to do so.

Key points

- Your puppy may begin teething at any time after you get him, so provide toys he can chew on for entertainment, comfort and to help his adult teeth come through. Otherwise, he may destroy your furniture and carpets.

- Do not give your puppy an old slipper or shoe to play with, because this could lead to inappropriate chewing. He will simply view all footwear as items to be shredded.

- Do not use sticks or lumps of wood as playthings. Splinters can cause injury, while sticks have a nasty habit of spearing dogs. Invest in good-quality toys that are durable and safe – rubber Kongs are good choices.

Teaching patience

Don't let your puppy demand attention any time he wants it. If he does, perhaps by jumping up or pawing at you, gently push him away.

You should ignore him until he stops bothering you and remains quiet.

Now you can reward him for being quiet, patient and undemanding. Through the use of food motivation and reward, your puppy will learn that he gets attention when you want to give it, *not* when he demands it.

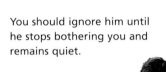

Sleep

For the first few weeks, your puppy's life will consist of eating and sleeping, intermingled with play. Although it is tempting to play endlessly with him, don't over-tire the youngster in the early, stressful days when he is settling into his new environment.

In his natural habitat, the puppy would regulate his own sleeping and waking times, so within reason you should try to maintain that pattern. Give him a bed in a quiet area of the house to which he can retreat and rest without being disturbed. Try to keep him active during the day so he will sleep at night.

Avoid getting up at night when the puppy cries. If he gets you up the first time he cries, he will learn that this behaviour gets attention – and you will be up every night!

Feeding

Your breeder should give you feeding instructions when you pick up your puppy, detailing the type of food he is being fed (this should be a puppy diet) and the daily quantity. As the puppy grows, consult your vet about the best diet for him.

Name training

1 One of the first things you will want to teach your puppy is to come to you when you call his name. Crouch down low and, in a warm tone and with an open gesture, call his name clearly and forcefully but without anger.

2 When the puppy comes to you, give him a treat and lavish praise. He will soon learn that he is well rewarded for coming to you when called. It really is as simple as that!

How to inspect your puppy's tummy

1 You can use food treats as an incentive to teach your pup to lie down and roll onto his side so you can inspect his tummy. Hold the treat where it will encourage the puppy to lie down – that is, down near the floor.

2 Move the treat over the puppy's shoulder so that he moves his head to follow it.

3 When you have moved the treat far enough, the puppy will flop on to his side, belly up. At this point, give him the treat and simultaneously stroke his tummy and praise him lavishly. Repeat the exercise and add a word command such as 'tummy' so the puppy learns what you want and will perform the action automatically.

Health care

Vaccination • First inoculations are usually done when the puppy is eight weeks old; consult your vet about which vaccinations he will need and when they should be given. Thereafter, the dog should have yearly boosters.

Parasite control • Find out from the puppy's breeder when he was last wormed and treated for other parasites, so that you can keep up with treatment in the early months. Your vet will advise on and supply the most suitable and effective treatments for internal and external parasites.

Neutering • There are sound reasons for neutering pet dogs, including:

• Helping to promote a more equable and gentle disposition.
• Reducing instances of disease and contracting illness. In some cases, neutering may become necessary on health grounds.
• Preventing unwanted pregnancies, therefore reducing the number of unwanted dogs.
• Helping to prevent roaming problems in male dogs and to reduce aggressive tendencies in both sexes.

However, neutering is always something that should be discussed with a vet, taking into account each individual dog's character, health, and also his position within the household pack if there is more than one dog involved.

If taught gently but firmly early in his life, your puppy will allow you to handle all areas of his body without stress to either you or him.

Play training

If you turn training into a game, your puppy will respond wonderfully. Try to channel play with your puppy into what will become recall and retrieve exercises at a later stage. If he brings a toy to you and drops it or gives it to you, reward him. You can also use toys to gain your puppy's attention. Show him that if he wants the toy, he will have to work for it.

If your puppy spontaneously offers behaviours you want, you can use the opportunity to further his training. For example, when he eliminates outside, be quick to praise and reward him; if he lies down beside you without pestering you for attention, reward him.

Handling

Your puppy must defer to you, his owner, or he will get the upper hand and be more difficult to handle as he matures. A dog generally dislikes having his eyes, mouth, paws, ears, tummy and anal area inspected. However, you and your vet or dog groomer need to be able to touch and inspect these areas easily if they require attention. Handle your puppy from an early age, being as gentle as possible so the experience is not unpleasant.

Key points

- Allow your puppy to settle into his new environment quietly; don't expect too much of him too soon.

- Make sure your puppy has a private area to retreat to for undisturbed rest whenever he wants.

- Puppies are very motivated by food, so treats are extremely useful training aids, as are toys, attention and praise.

- Do not give in to attention-seeking behaviour.

- Handle the puppy from day one to accustom him to being touched and inspected all over.

Carrying a puppy

1 Crouch down and gently but firmly gather the puppy to you as shown, with one arm around his chest to keep him from breaking free and the other arm under his bottom for support.

2 Keeping the puppy close to your body so that he feels safe and secure and can't jump from your arms, stand up slowly.

3 Carry the puppy close to your chest. To put him down, simply reverse the actions. Throughout, bend from the knees to avoid straining your back.

1 Collar and leash training

Key points

- Walk the puppy on your left side with a slack leash; keeping it taut will encourage him to pull against or resist it.

- Remember to train little and often, or the puppy will become bored and restless. Always finish on a positive note.

- Make training a game so the puppy will think it is fun, not a chore.

- Check collar fit regularly as your puppy grows.

- Once your puppy is leash trained, you can start attending puppy socializing classes.

You would think that walking a puppy on a leash was simple, wouldn't you? Put on the collar and leash, and off you go. However, if these items are not introduced correctly, leash training can be difficult and traumatic for both of you.

First, put the collar on the puppy for short periods, praising him lavishly as you do so. Then distract him with a game or treat so that he gets used to the feel of something around his neck and associates it with a pleasant experience.

Once your puppy is happy with the collar, clip on a short leash and let him follow you around the house for short periods. Again, be generous with praise and rewards. Once he is completely happy, you can start to teach your puppy to walk by your side while you are holding the leash.

Leash training

1 Hold the leash in your right hand and a reward (a treat or favourite toy) in your left, and move it around to get the puppy interested in it.

2 Walk backwards and call the puppy's name; keep the leash slack and entice him with the reward. If he is reluctant to follow, let him mouth the toy or give him a taste of the treat, call his name again and continue backing away. He will now be sure to come with you.

Leading on the left

The reason for walking your puppy on your left, with the leash across your body and held in your right hand, is that most people are right-handed. This is the stronger side, so if the dog is walked on the left side and pulls forward, the owner's body is better balanced to control the pull. In addition, the hand closest to the puppy is left free to hold a treat or toy and coax him as necessary.

The idea of using a half-check collar (see Correct Equipment panel, right) is to attract the puppy's attention with the rattling of the chain portion, but because the rest of the collar is made of fabric it will not damage his neck. When you use your right hand to check the puppy and produce the sound, the leash goes across your body to make the rattle without choking the puppy. If you hold the leash on the same side as the puppy, you will pull against his bodyweight and choke him.

(see Correct Equipment panel, right)

Correct equipment

Collar
Choose a 'kind' collar such as a half-check (shown here) or a broad collar in leather or nylon, the appropriate weight and width for the puppy's size. When it

is fitted, you should be able to get two or three fingers underneath it: if it is too loose, it may slip off; if too tight, it will cause discomfort, especially when the puppy is eating or drinking. When a half-check is pulled tight, there should be a minimum of two links of chain between the two D rings.

This type of collar is designed so that when the puppy is checked, the chain rattles and gains his attention. It is definitely *not* designed to cause uncomfortable tension around the puppy's tender neck.

Leash
Leash type is important. First, it must be comfortable for you to hold. Next, it must be of a suitable length to maintain slack tension. A retractable nylon leash that can be lengthened or retracted will give you the best of both worlds.

3 Once the puppy is happily walking towards you, bring the hand with the treat around towards your leg and then forward, and he will turn to follow it.

4 Walk forwards, rewarding the puppy as you do so. Use the commands 'walk' and 'heel', so that he learns to associate the actions with the command and reward.

5 Note the correct way to hold the leash and the correct position for the puppy by your side.

6 During initial leash training, keep a toy or treat in your left hand so that if the puppy becomes distracted, starts pulling or lags behind, you can entice him back to the correct position and pace, then reward him.

2 Making new friends

Imagine a world where you cannot speak the language, where you are afraid of someone walking towards you on the street, or where meeting a group of people terrifies you. Without realizing it, you can turn your dog into a nervous wreck simply by not socializing him correctly for such situations as a puppy.

It is during the sixth and seventh weeks of life that puppies in a litter learn the finer points of social skills in their family environment. Once you take your puppy home, you are responsible for introducing him into your world. This is the only way he can discover how to socialize with other dogs, be well-mannered when meeting people in the street, and learn when enough is enough during play.

Handling your puppy while he's eating will help ensure that he doesn't become possessive about food. Adding more food to the bowl mid-meal teaches him that someone handling his food represents a reward, not a threat.

Accustom your puppy to meeting and being with people of all ages and both sexes, and reward him so that he views their company as a good thing.

Key points

- Do not let your puppy jump up at people, or allow them to let him. Give him attention only if he waits patiently to be petted.

- Introduce him to household sights and sounds, such as the television, radio, washing machine and so on, one at a time over a period of days.

- Expose your puppy to different outdoor

sights and sounds gradually, so he is not overwhelmed.

- Get the puppy used to car travel as soon as possible, beginning with short trips, but make sure he is secure in the vehicle. It's best to put him in a crate with his blanket for comfort and a toy to distract him.

When introducing your puppy to older dogs, start with a good-natured one that will play with the youngster and not intimidate him.

Sights and sounds

Your puppy needs to become accustomed to traffic noise so he won't be frightened by it when you are walking him. Get him used to both day and night walking so he becomes oblivious to headlights as well as the noise and sight of vehicles.

If your puppy has a problem with this, find a quiet stretch of road where you can spend some time just sitting and watching the world go by. Each time a vehicle approaches, distract your puppy by showing him a treat, then when the vehicle has passed, let him have it. This way he will come to associate traffic with getting a reward.

Other animals

You also need to accustom your puppy to other animals, including cats, rabbits, guinea pigs, hamsters, caged birds, cattle, horses, sheep – in fact, anything to which you can introduce him. Again, use food rewards as a distraction if the puppy becomes excited or frightened. Then reward him for being quiet and calm when he is around other animals.

TRAINER'S TIP

To help accustom the puppy to other animals in the household, put his bedding in with the other animal for a while to transfer its scent, then put the blanket back in the puppy's bed. He will learn to recognize the animal's scent as familiar and comforting.

Puppy training classes

Once your puppy has been vaccinated, the best way to socialize him is to take him to puppy training classes held in a secure area. There he can meet other puppies of his own age and size, as well as other people.

Allowed to intermingle – first on the leash, then loose – the puppies will quickly find an acceptable level of chase and play and sort out the pecking order among themselves. It is important in these initial stages that they are not forced into a frightening situation. A good trainer will ensure that play-fighting doesn't get out of hand and will prevent any bullying.

3 Crate training

Training your puppy to use a crate happily will come in very handy. Also known as a den, pen or cage, a crate serves as a bed and a quiet, secure place to which your puppy can retreat. It also keeps the puppy (and later the adult dog) separate from people when necessary, is useful for toilet training, and is a safe place to put him when travelling in a vehicle.

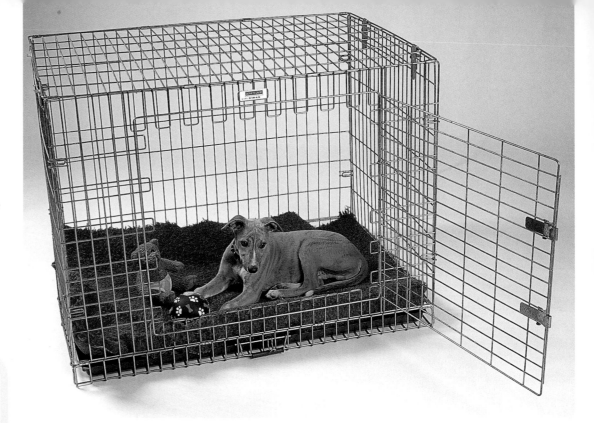

TRAINER'S TIP

Gradually increase the period of time for which the puppy is left in the crate while you are at home, from a few minutes to up to half an hour. At four or five months of age and older, he will recognize it as a 'safety zone' and happily stay there overnight or while you are at work.

A crate can be a great tool for toilet training, but remember that you should only leave the puppy in the crate for extended periods after he has eaten and been outside to exercise and take care of bathroom needs. Otherwise, he may need to urinate or defecate in the crate. Since dogs dislike soiling in or near their beds, having to relieve himself in the crate could make your puppy unwilling to stay inside it.

It is important to introduce your puppy to a crate correctly, or he may come to view it as a prison rather than a pleasant, safe place to be.

To start, use toys and treats to encourage your puppy to go into the crate, leaving the door open so he can go in and out as he wants. Put the crate in a quiet but not isolated area of the house so the puppy won't be disturbed when he's inside but at the same time will not feel abandoned. Be careful not to place it in direct sunlight or in areas that get too hot or too cold.

Crates come in all sizes, with various types of openings. Choose one that will be big enough for your puppy when he is fully grown. A two-door foldaway crate is especially convenient for use in a vehicle. Put comfy, familiar bedding and the puppy's favourite toys in the crate to encourage him to go inside and feel at home. The best time to do this initially is after a play session, when he is tired and ready for a rest.

Accustom the puppy to going in and staying in the crate by feeding him there, but with the door open at first so he doesn't feel trapped. Once he is used to this and willingly goes in at mealtimes, feed him with the door closed for short periods, then gradually extend the time. Remember, though, that puppies generally need to relieve themselves after eating, so he will have to go outside soon.

Help the puppy learn that the crate is a nice place to be by giving him a filled activity toy such as a stuffed Kong (see pages 31 and 32), which will keep him pleasurably occupied.

Key points

- Never use a crate as a 'punishment pen'.

- Plastic-covered metal crates are quieter and easier to clean than those constructed of bare or galvanized metal.

- To give the puppy extra privacy or encourage him to be quiet (providing he isn't crying to go outside), cover the crate with a blanket.

- You can use a crate as a portable kennel when visiting or on vacation. For safety, you can keep your puppy in the crate when introducing him to other household pets.

- Once he is used to a crate, a puppy that is prone to chewing furniture, carpets and other inappropriate objects can be removed from temptation until the behaviour has been resolved.

4 Toilet training

Puppies need to be taught appropriate bathroom habits; they *do not* do this naturally. You can expect a few accidents at first, so keep the pup in areas where it doesn't matter if he deposits the odd pile or puddle.

Be prepared at first to take your puppy for lots of outside visits at the appropriate times. Just like human babies, young dogs need to relieve themselves quite frequently until they gain fuller control over their natural bodily functions.

Key points ☑

- Don't expect a young puppy to be clean in the house overnight or throughout the day if shut inside. If you do catch him in the act, scoop him up and take him outside to the bathroom area.

- Never shout at or smack your puppy if he has an accident; he won't understand why you are angry and will simply become frightened of you.

- Never rub a puppy's nose in his mess in the belief that this will stop him from soiling in the house. It won't, and you will only scare him.

- Praise and reward lavishly when the puppy relieves himself outside so he learns that it is well worth repeating.

- Always take the puppy outside to his bathroom area after waking, eating and playing.

- After eating and going outside, the longest a young puppy can be left in a crate during the day is three to four hours; at night, he should be confined for no more than five to six hours. In any case, leaving a puppy in a crate longer than this is very unfair.

- You must learn to recognize the signals when your puppy needs to relieve himself. He may pace the floor, refusing to settle, or whine and go to the door. Sometimes puppies will seek a private place to go such as behind furniture, so be watchful for this.

Until your puppy is completely toilet trained, it is a good idea to put down newspaper in the area he inhabits so that messes are easier to clean up.

Teaching appropriate habits

1 A puppy usually needs to relieve himself after eating and playing, so these are the times to take him outside to his designated bathroom area, which should be marked off with a length of rope or hosepipe to define it clearly.

2 Wait until the puppy relieves himself, then praise him so he knows that his actions in that place were desirable.

3 Leaving the puppy's last droppings there will indicate to him by sight and smell that this is the right place to go.

Using crate training

Crate training (see pages 44–45) comes in handy when toilet training your puppy, but do not leave a young pup in a crate all day or night and expect him to be clean. He won't be able to contain himself and will end up distressed because he has soiled his bed. You must be able to take the puppy out to relieve himself at regular intervals or arrange for someone else to do so.

TRAINER'S TIP

Your puppy will almost certainly need to relieve himself after he wakes up, so this is another good time to take him outside.

Cleaning up

Accidents do happen. When cleaning up faeces, urine or vomit, avoid using household cleaners that contain ammonia, a component of excretions. The lingering smell will encourage the puppy to soil the same spot again.

Instead, use commercial pet-stain cleaners (available from pet stores) on soiled areas in the house. These products eliminate odours so your puppy won't be attracted to the same spot.

5 Play-biting

Puppies love to bite and chew things because it helps them teethe. In addition, play-biting or fighting is part of the instinctive canine learning process for hunting, food-gathering and establishing status in the pack.

Your puppy will treat you like a pack member while he is learning social skills, but you must help teach him (just as his mother would) exactly what constitutes appropriate and inappropriate behaviour. Play-biting most certainly represents the latter.

If encouraged or left unchecked, play-biting becomes increasingly severe, until the dog is of a size and age where he really hurts and frightens human 'targets', especially children. You must teach your puppy that biting is unacceptable.

Key points

- Instead of your hand or arm, give the puppy toys that he can chew and play with without harming anyone.

- Yelp loudly if the puppy tries to bite you. Move away from him and ignore him until he leaves you alone, then reward him with attention for not persisting in biting. This imitates the actions his mother and littermates would take to discourage rough play.

- Do not encourage the puppy to play-bite, and be very strict about not allowing children to let him bite them in play.

- Do not tap the puppy's nose when he bites; it will just encourage him to continue biting.

- Handle your puppy's mouth from day one so he becomes accustomed to hands being in and around his jaws without biting (see pages 37 and 39). Praise the puppy for letting you do this, so he learns that he is rewarded for not biting.

Discouraging biting

1 Spray a non-toxic, bitter-tasting liquid (available from pet stores) on the areas of your body that the puppy frequently tries to bite – usually hands and arms.

TRAINER'S TIP

You can also use repellent spray for pets to discourage your puppy from chewing on household items (such as table legs, shoes and so on).

2 Hold out your hand and let the puppy mouth it.

3 The puppy will usually recoil in disgust at the foul taste. In this way, after a number of repetitions, he will learn that biting humans is unpleasant.

Noisy discouragement

Puppies don't like loud or sudden noises, so you can use such sounds to discourage play-biting.

Half-fill a small container with a tight lid with pebbles and shake it hard when the puppy tries to bite you.

He will react in surprise at the noise and will back away from you.

When he does, leave him for a moment to settle down, then go to him and give him attention. This way, he learns that biting results in an unpleasant shock, while not biting is rewarded.

6 Jumping up

Puppies jump up at humans in greeting; in the wild, dogs instinctively greet returning pack members by sniffing and licking at their mouths to try to get them to regurgitate or drop food.

Since the mouth is a rewarding area of the body, puppies jump up at us in an attempt to reach it. We must teach them that this is not rewarding, so never respond to the puppy when he jumps up.

Although a little puppy jumping into your arms may seem truly adorable, just imagine how you would cope with such behaviour when he is fully grown. Even if you don't mind him almost knocking you over as he plants two muddy paws on your shoulders, he could pose a real danger to other people such as pregnant women, frail or elderly people and children when out on walks.

1 If your puppy jumps up at someone, tell her to fold her arms so that they are out of his reach, turn away to avoid eye contact, and ignore his actions.

Key points

- Most people, especially children, love to say hello to puppies (and adult dogs) when out walking, but it is important that you ask them to refrain from doing so until the puppy sits and waits quietly for attention.

- Always ignore the puppy when he jumps up.

- When the puppy is trying to get attention, avoid eye contact and acknowledge him only when he has settled down and has all four paws on the ground.

- Give the puppy attention only if you have first called him to you.

- When you have finished petting him, say 'enough' and gently push him away, fold your arms, avoid eye contact and ignore him.

- Play with the puppy only if you initiate the contact. Let him know when you have finished, as described above.

- Make sure visitors know and follow your rules for giving the puppy attention, and tell them what to do if he jumps up at them.

2 The person should continue to ignore the puppy until he stays down, which he will eventually do when he does not get any reaction.

3 The person should wait until the puppy settles down and makes no further attempt to approach or jump up.

4 Now the person should reward the puppy with attention and praise. This teaches him that jumping up is a negative experience, while not doing so is a positive one.

5 Practise this exercise at home and out on walks, until when someone approaches your puppy he makes no attempt to seek attention from or jump up at them. Only then should the person acknowledge the puppy.

TRAINER'S TIP

It is not fair to allow your dog to jump up at you as a puppy and then scold him for doing so when he grows into a big dog. He will be confused by your inconsistent reactions.

7 Food training

Food is very important to dogs, and they can become possessive about it. In the litter, puppies fight over the best teat in order to get as much food as their bellies will hold, and they do the same with solid food after weaning. This behaviour is instinctive and relates to their experience in the wild of never knowing when their next meal will be or where it will come from.

Establishing pack hierarchy

Pack rule is that the highest-ranking members eat first, then allow the lower-ranking ones to feed. This rule must also apply in your household, or the puppy will assert himself as number one – and not just at mealtimes!

You need to teach your puppy that it is not necessary to fight for food and that a human near his food bowl does not constitute a threat to his meal. You must also assert yourself as pack leader so the puppy eats only how and when you dictate.

Permission to eat

1 Have your puppy on the leash and put down his food bowl.

Do not allow the puppy to eat, using the leash to restrain him as necessary, along with the command 'leave'. Encourage him to sit, or at least stand, quietly by your side.

2 Wait until the puppy looks at you for permission to eat, although this may take a while. Eventually the puppy will look to you to see whether you are ready to let him eat.

3 When he does this, say 'eat' and allow him to do so. Praise him for his patience.

4 As the puppy is eating, add a treat or two to the bowl so that he views hands near his food as non-threatening.

Key points

• If there are children in the household, supervise them to carry out the same training, so that the puppy also views them as being of higher rank.

• Do this exercise at every mealtime until the puppy will wait off-leash until he is told to eat.

• Once the puppy associates the 'leave' command with leaving food alone until he has been given permission to have it, you can use the same command for other things, such as items that he chews.

• While the puppy is waiting to eat, move away from him and use the command 'wait' or 'stay', which he will do because he is unwilling to move away from the food. Then return to the puppy, praise him and allow him to eat.

• Using these methods, you will be able to teach the puppy to leave things alone and to stay and wait where you want him. The simple ideas are always the best!

WEEKEND OBEDIENCE TRAINING:
11 essentials for the adult dog

Training plan

Weekend 1: Sit
Lie down
Roll over
Stay

Weekend 2: Socializing
House manners

Weekend 3: Away
Retrieve
Recall

As we have seen, the key to owning a well-trained dog is to start him on the right track when he is a puppy. But what happens if you acquire an adult dog, one who hasn't been trained or whose manners leave something to be desired?

Training adult dogs

Choose the area(s) of obedience that you would most like to improve, either from choice or necessity, and work on those first. However, bear in mind that if you want to improve, say, recall, then your dog must already be responsive to his name; if he isn't, then you will need to teach him this first. The same applies for road safety – if your dog is not used to being on a leash, or has no leash manners, then you will have to teach him to behave appropriately as the first step.

All areas of obedience training require continual reinforcement to ensure that both you and your dog stay sharp. Read the detailed step-by-step instructions on how to teach these exercises in the following pages.

Some areas of obedience may be initiated in the same weekend, as they naturally complement each other. Three groups of such related areas are:
• Sit, lie down, roll ove and stay
• Socializing and house manners
• Away, retrieve and recall
Otherwise, try to initiate training in separate weekends to avoid confusing your dog.
The Training Plan above is an example timetable of what can be achieved in three weekends of intensive training, comprising eight 15-minute sessions per day, plus continual reinforcement of all exercises during daily walks and playtime. It is based on a fit, healthy adult dog of average intelligence with no behavioural problems, who already knows his name.

Work out a plan based on your dog's needs for 10–15 minutes maximum of concentrated training in a one-hour session, plus additional play and exercise time for light relief and fun. Break down the areas of obedience training you want to work

Key points

• Some dogs take longer than others to grasp what you are trying to teach.

• Patience and remaining relaxed reap rewards.

• Remember: little and often is best. Keep training sessions short, and always finish on a positive note.

• Reward all desirable behaviours.

• Attending regular training sessions will be beneficial for you and your dog.

With time and correct training, developing a well-trained dog is not as difficult as you may think.

All dogs are different

Some dogs learn faster than others. Large breeds tend to mature more slowly, so you need to be extra-patient with them sometimes. Small dogs, on the other hand, can be too clever for their own good, and you will have to be on your toes!

Bear in mind that working breeds, while intelligent, have an inbred instinct to chase and retrieve, guard or herd – or all three – so they require disciplined handling and training to get the very best from them. Some owners may find such dogs too much of a handful.

If you own a dog like this and really cannot commit to or give him the type of training and exercise he needs, you need to consider your options. Finding the dog a home with someone who can offer the type of environment and training he needs is not a failure on your part: rather, it is a selfless act that will give the dog a chance to lead a more fulfilled and happier life.

on into a progressive programme, moving on to the next stage only once you have achieved the results you require.

Good manners

The following pages explain how you can train your adult dog in the basics of good manners, from walking to heel on the leash and coming to you when you call him, to sitting, staying and behaving well in the house.

Some people take these things for granted, expecting a dog to know automatically what is required of him, but that simply isn't the case. You wouldn't expect a new employee to know the job on the first day, and it's the same for a new dog. He has to get to know you and your way of doing things, while you have to get to know him and find out what makes him tick.

Food rewards and praise are the most effective ways to elicit a favourable response from dogs. Rewarding desired behaviours will soon have your dog behaving the way you want him to – even in a weekend!

Good instruction

Keep a diary so that you can see how things are going, and note down areas of particular achievement or difficulty so you can work on the exercises that your dog finds more testing. Above all, stay calm, be patient and make training fun.

Finding a good trainer will be invaluable in helping you turn your dog into a well-mannered and controllable companion. Regular training sessions will help point you in the right direction, as well as being enjoyable. Many trainers will also give you and your dog the chance to try various activities such as agility, flyball, scenting work and the increasingly popular heelwork to music.

So, although this book shows you how to go about doing things the right way, remember that additional on-the-spot help and advice can be invaluable when it comes to putting what you have learned into practice.

1 Name response

Teaching your dog his name

If you get your dog as an adult, he is likely to already have a name, which he may or may not know. If he has learned that responding to his name is unrewarding, you have two choices: change his name to one you prefer and teach him to respond to it, or re-train him to respond to his existing name.

When choosing a name, pick one that's short and rolls off your tongue in one or two syllables. This way, it is easy to say quickly, and the dog will soon learn to recognize it. Beyond this, naming your dog is a matter of personal choice.

Homework

Once you have brought your new dog home from his rescue centre or previous owner's home, you will need to start from the beginning. Do not assume that the dog is aware of his name or that he is used to being called by it.

Let your dog find his way around his new home. Once he has investigated his surroundings, you can start to ask him to come to you. Call him by his name and add the command 'come'. When the dog reacts to your voice, entice him to you with encouraging words, and as he reaches you give him a treat or praise.

Initially, try to attract the dog's attention to you by calling him; if this fails, you can revert to treat training. You can also add treat training to speed up the process.

1 When you begin name training, work in a secure area so that the dog cannot escape your control, or have him on a long leash. Opening your arms to indicate a friendly welcome, call the dog's name enthusiastically to get his attention.

2 As your dog looks at you, offer a food reward – a tasty treat that he cannot resist – or his favourite toy.

3 Call the dog again and crouch down so that you do not appear intimidating, especially to a small or nervous dog. When he comes to you, give him a treat or toy and praise him lavishly. With this method, your dog will learn that coming to you when you call his name is very rewarding.

Key points

- Do not always put your dog on the leash when he comes to you in response to his name. Instead, play with his collar and handle his neck. Then release him with the command 'away' or 'go play'. Repeat this exercise often, so the dog associates coming to you with play, not with loss of freedom.

- Remember that your dog's name is just that: it is *not* a command. Many people shout the dog's name and expect him to sit or to walk with them without a command. The dog can only do what you ask him to do, so tell him what you want.

- Always remain calm when calling your dog. If he doesn't respond, ask yourself if he actually knows what you want. Have you demonstrated things clearly enough for him to understand?

- If the dog doesn't respond to his name, stop, take a break and try again later. Never call his name in anger; he will be unlikely to come to you if he generally associates that tone with an unpleasant experience.

2 Leash manners

Taking your dog for a walk is pleasurable and relaxing for both of you – if he is leash trained correctly. If your dog is not accustomed to a collar or leash, turn to pages 40–41 for advice on how to get started.

Common problems

A common problem encountered on walks is the dog getting ahead or even pulling his owner along, anxious to get on with the walk and reach wherever he is going.

Conversely, the dog may lag behind, or need to be dragged away from a patch of grass he is intent on sniffing.

TRAINER'S TIP

It is essential to check a retractable leash regularly to be sure it is in good working order. Also, the leash shold be able to take the weight of your dog if he bolts and you have to stop him quickly.

This is the ideal: the dog walking attentively and calmly at his owner's side. To achieve this, follow the steps on pages 60–61.

(follow the steps on pages 60–61.)

Don't forget

Always clean up after your dog if he defecates while on a walk. You can buy a special scoop and bags at pet stores, or simply carry a plastic bag in your pocket. Put the waste in a receptacle designed for the purpose (if available), double-bag it and place in a normal street waste bin, or take it home and dispose of it there.

Fitting a headcollar

The correct use of a headcollar will prove invaluable when training your dog to walk with you. It allows you to apply gentle pressure on the leash that will turn the dog's head away from possible distractions.

This headcollar is too small for the dog: it is too high on the nose and close to the eyes.

This headcollar fits correctly.

To fit a headcollar, slip the noseband over the dog's nose as shown.

Position the headpiece around the back of the head, gently lifting the dog's ears out of the way.

Finally, fasten the headcollar.

Walking to heel

1 Begin with the dog on your left side, with his shoulder against your left leg and the leash held in your right hand as shown. Say your dog's name to get his attention, then 'heel'.

2 Begin walking purposefully.

3 If the dog walks in front of you or pulls, stop. He will no doubt look back at you in surprise.

Training to heel

At first, use the command 'heel' only when your dog is in the required position, so he learns the word by association. Reinforce the command with a reward (praise or a treat) so the dog learns that this position is a pleasant one in which to remain. Once he has learned where 'heel' is you can use the command to return him to that position.

Keeping up the pace

If your dog often lags behind it could be because:

• He is more interested in sniffing to identify who else has been along that way previously, and possibly in marking his own passage.

• You are walking too fast for him to keep up.

4 Guide him back into position and

a.
or
In
are sh
difficult

Key points

- Always remain alert when walking your dog so you are prepared for all eventualities, such as your dog suddenly jumping up at passers-by or trying to run after another animal.

- Don't be lazy: be sure you keep your dog at heel on all walks to reinforce his training.

- Some dogs do better on walks if they wear a headcollar rather than just a collar.

- Keep treats or a toy in
  dog is

'Follow my pack leader'

Another method of keeping your dog's attention on you is by reinforcing your control. In order to do this, play 'follow my pack leader'.

1 Walk along as usual, with the dog by your left side.

2 Suddenly swing your left leg around and in front of your dog.

4 Reward the dog with a treat, or a verbal reward such as 'good dog'. Repeat whenever you need to reinforce your control.

3 Sit

Having your dog in the sit position is the starting point for further essential training, such as lie down and stay. Four principles apply to training your dog to sit on command, and they may also be applied to heel training. The acronym ACER will help you remember them.

1 Attention
2 Command
3 Execute
4 Reward

Treat training

If you wish to use treats to train your dog to sit, follow the instructions below:

1 Stand beside your dog with the leash in your left hand, the dog on your right hand side and a treat in your right hand.

2 Offer the treat, then give the command 'sit' and at the same time move the treat up towards the dog's nose and over his head.

3 Move the treat back slightly so the dog is looking up.

4 He will automatically move into the sit position.

5 As he does, reward him with the treat.

Teaching him to sit

1 Stand with your dog on your left side, with the leash and a treat in your right hand, and get his **attention** by saying his name.

2 Command 'sit' and simultaneously apply gentle pressure with your left hand on the dog's rear end to push him down.

3 Responding to the pressure, the dog will **execute** the command by sitting.

4 When he does so, **reward** him with the treat.

Key points ✓

- Be patient when teaching the sit: dogs feel vulnerable in this position.

- When rewarding with a treat, do not hold it so high that the dog tries to jump up to get it. He will associate the reward with jumping instead of the required sit position.

- Always request that your dog sits before feeding him or putting on his leash.

- When you are out walking and want your dog to sit, slow down, then put him in the sit position.

- Remember: ACER!

Using a clicker

A clicker is a small hand-held tool that can be used to 'condition' good behaviour. It is simple but effective: just press and click.

The great thing about the clicker is that it is instantaneous; the moment the dog displays a desired behaviour, click, then reward with a treat. The dog learns that the sound means a particular behaviour is required, and this is reinforced by the reward. Click, reward; no click, no reward. Being clever, dogs soon get the idea.

Another good thing about a clicker is that you can use it at a distance, and the dog will come to you for his expected reward. A clicker is also suitable for training puppies.

1 Stand with your dog and wait until he sits.

2 As soon as he does, click and say 'sit' (and/or use a hand signal).

3 Reward him with a treat and praise.

4 Lie down and roll over

Once your dog has learned to sit, as explained on pages 62–63, the next step is to teach him to lie down on command, then roll onto his side.

Being able to have your dog lie down on command, then roll over and let you handle him all over, is extremely handy for grooming, visits to the vet, or just having him lie quietly while you are occupied with something else.

1 With your dog in the sit position, get him to focus his attention on a treat in your hand.

2 Put the treat under his nose, then slowly move it down to the floor or between his front paws. He will sink to the floor in his effort to get the treat. As soon as he does, say 'down' and reward with the treat and praise. Practise this a couple of times and you will find that your dog soon learns to lie down on command in anticipation of a reward.

TRAINER'S TIP

• To teach your dog to sit up and then stand from a lying position, put a treat under his nose and raise it above his head, simultaneously saying 'sit' or 'stand'. Reward him for the desired response with a treat.

• Practise each exercise separately at first and reward after each element. Then request a sit, down, stay, and follow with a reward. Finally, request all of these and a stand after the stay, then give a reward. This usually turns out to be a game that the dog really enjoys.

3 If all goes well try extending the lie down into a stay. As you step away from the lying dog, say 'stay' (with a hand signal as shown, if necessary), wait a couple of seconds, then go back to the dog and reward him lavishly. Gradually extend the distance between you and your dog as you command the stay. You will be surprised at how quickly he learns to do this, too.

Key points

- Instant reward is essential to teach these exercises effectively because a dog is at his most vulnerable in a lying position. A reward will take his mind off that feeling and teach him that lying on command is pleasant and non-threatening.

- Be patient: if you get annoyed, the dog will sense it, and you are unlikely to achieve your goal. Some dogs take longer than others to feel at ease with these exercises.

- Always finish the exercise on a positive note. If the dog gets bored, stop and ask him to do something he knows and enjoys, then reward so the lesson ends well. You can always try again tomorrow.

Roll over

With your dog in the down position, you can move on to the roll-over exercise. Because exposing his tummy makes him feel vulnerable to potential attackers, your dog will lie on his side or back only if he feels safe and secure. You must teach this exercise carefully if you are to be successful and avoid stress to your dog. Attempt it only when both of you are relaxed and at ease with each other.

1 Show your dog a treat.

2 Move the treat closer to the dog's nose, then move it slowly around towards his shoulder, over the back of his neck and down.

3 The dog's head will follow your hand until he has to lie flat on his side to keep the treat in sight.

4 At this point say 'roll over', give your dog the treat and stroke his tummy. Practise until he learns that 'roll over' is a rewarding command to follow.

5 Stay

The ability to get your dog to stay where you want him, both indoors and out, is often very useful. For instance, you can use this command if you have visitors and you want the dog to remain in his bed out of the way, or if he needs to stay put for his own safety and that of others while on a walk.

Key points

- Always stay close to your dog as you move around him at first so he knows you are still there.

- Don't forget that the dog will get bored very quickly if you continue to practise the same thing over and over. If you get a positive result on the first attempt, don't repeat it. Finish on that good note.

- To release the dog from the sit-stay, say the dog's name and then 'here', adopting a welcoming posture to encourage him to come to you. Reward him when he does so.

- Dogs read body language well and will notice when you are bored with the training session, so stay alert and maintain the dog's attention.

Teaching him to stay

1 Put the dog into the sit position by your left heel.

2 Walk around the dog with him in a controlled stay, so command 'stay', with the leash slack in your left hand. Hold your right hand with the palm open in front of your dog as a visual signal. Repeat the 'stay' command and then take one step out to the side of the dog.

TRAINER'S TIP

Stay can be difficult for a rescue dog to learn because he may feel that he is being abandoned. The best advice is to be patient and stay close to him until he realizes that you are not leaving him.

3 Repeat the command, then walk briskly around the dog, staying close to him so he knows where you are.

4 When you complete the circuit, you should be standing by your dog's right side. Reward with gentle, calm praise and a treat if desired. Repeat the exercise, this time moving a little further away at the front but coming close again at the back.

5 You will be able to develop the stay further as the dog becomes more confident that you are not abandoning him and is comfortable with staying put. Extend the leash and increase the distance as you walk in front of the dog and around him.

Free stay

Once you are happy with your dog staying put, you can progress to the free stay. Move away from your dog, command 'stay' and drop the leash on the floor. Wait a few seconds, then walk back to and around the dog, finishing by his right side. Reward him with a treat.

6 Away

This command is very useful for sending your dog to his bed or crate or away from something you don't want him near. The method of teaching it is simple but extremely effective.

Using treats to teach 'away'

1 Slice some really tasty treats, such as hot dogs, into small pieces. Put them in a plastic container with a lid and show them to your dog.

The command 'away' can be used to send a dog out of the room.

TRAINER'S TIP

Always finish on a positive note, so the dog remembers a pleasant experience with the away command.

2 Using the 'away' command, guide the dog to his bed (or out of the room), reward him, and place the container of treats next to him so he can see them.

3 Because the treats are so close to him, the dog will be reluctant to leave his position. Reinforce this with a 'stay' command and reward him again. In this way, he will come to regard wherever he is as a nice place to be.

4 Continue with whatever it is that you want to do while your dog is away from you. If he comes to you without being called, simply repeat the exercise, using 'away' as you put him back in his bed or out of the room.

Key points

- Keep the exercise short to start with, so the dog doesn't become bored and switch off.

- Ignore your dog if he comes back to you uninvited; then return him to the position in which you left him, again using the away command.

- At first, don't wait too long before calling the dog back to you, or he will get bored and come looking for you.

- Practise this exercise often so your dog learns by reward association that 'away' is a good command to obey.

7 Road safety

Knowing how to cross a road correctly with your dog is vital for everyone's safety. He should cross *with* you, not be dragged across by you, or vice versa. There is obvious danger in an owner struggling across a road with a dog who is out of control.

In order to be able to cross a road safely, your dog must obey the 'sit' command. If you need to review this, see pages 62–63. Only when your dog is sitting calmly and quietly by your side can you concentrate fully on the traffic to be sure the road is absolutely clear before you cross. An ill-trained dog is a danger not only to himself and you, but also to drivers and other pedestrians.

TRAINER'S TIP

Using a retractable leash isn't a good idea when walking your dog next to traffic. If he should dash out into the path of vehicles you may not be able to stop him quickly enough.

Crossing safely

1 If your dog is not used to traffic, accustom him to the sights and sounds by taking him to a spot where you can sit and watch traffic go by without being too close. Distract him by offering small pieces of food or a desirable toy. Do not fuss over him too much or hold on to him; that will just make him feel that there is something to be afraid of. Speak to him calmly and in a normal tone.

2 Once the dog appears to be not bothered by the traffic, walk him quietly along the pavement, again distracting him as vehicles approach. Reward him once they have passed. Soon he will look to you for a reward and take no notice of the traffic.

- Start by training on quiet roads.

- Ensure that your dog's collar is adjusted correctly so he can't slip out of it and escape into the road.

- Leash length is important. It must be a suitable type for the size of your dog and not too long for good handling and control.

- Keep your dog in the sit position as traffic is passing so he is under control until you are ready to cross.

- Be sure you have the dog's attention before stepping off the kerb to cross the road.

3 When crossing the road, stop at a point where you have a good view in both directions. Avoid crossing at corners and junctions, unless there is a pedestrian crossing. Command your dog to sit at the heel position while you check out whether the road is safe to cross. Continue to remind the dog to stay, keeping his attention on you with a treat, toy or verbal encouragement until you cross.

4 Cross only when the road is clear in both directions. Keep checking for approaching vehicles and keep your dog's attention on you by having a treat in the hand closest to him.

8 Retrieve

Throwing a toy for your dog to retrieve is a good way to see that he gets adequate exercise. It's also a game that both of you can enjoy, at least for as long as your arm holds out. But if a dog won't retrieve for you, how do you get him interested in playing 'fetch' in the first place?

High-value toys

First, you need to use a toy that you can take from the dog's mouth easily, without endangering your fingers. Suggestions include a Kong on a rope, a ball on a rope, a suitably sized rubber ring, a rope toy and a rubber tug toy. These are all 'high-value' toys because of their throw/chase/tug of war attributes.

It is important that you let your dog play with a high-value toy only when you have control of it. Play with your dog, then put the toy away when the game or training session is finished so the toy retains its 'special' status for the dog.

A rope toy, rubber ring and rubber tug toy.

Teaching him to retrieve

1 Use an everyday (low-value) toy as the item to be retrieved, but have the high-value toy in your pocket or hidden behind your back to use as the reward once your dog brings the other toy back to you. Have the dog at heel in a sit-stay position (see pages 63 and 66–67 to review these exercises) then throw the low-value toy, saying 'fetch' at the same time.

2 Once the dog has the toy, call him back to you by saying his name and 'fetch'.

TRAINER'S TIP

If you let your dog spit out the item or drop it at your feet, it may be a problem if you ever want to do fun obedience competitions with him. Train the dog to 'give' by releasing the toy into your hand right from the start.

3 When he comes to you, reward him with praise or a treat and the high-value toy. Repeat once or twice, and finish on a positive note.

4 If your dog will chase the toy but not bring it to you, show him the high-value toy to entice him. Most dogs cannot resist this.

5 Praise the dog lavishly when he returns with the low-value toy, then play a game with the high-value toy. Your dog will soon get the message: no low-value toy, no game.

6 Another ploy you can try when the dog won't bring his toy back to you is to walk away from him. Thinking he is being left, he will usually trot after you. When he does, drop down on one knee and call him to you, then give a treat when he comes. If that fails, simply turn your back on the dog; he will wonder why you are ignoring him and will come to you seeking reassurance. Reward him when he does.

(continued)

7 Once your dog has got the hang of retrieving the low-value toy, attach a long training leash, toss the high-value toy out a metre or two and say 'fetch'. The dog will almost certainly dash out and pick it up.

8 Next, you want the dog to bring the high-value toy back to you, at which point you can give him a reward. As he picks up the toy call 'fetch' again. He should then return to you. If he doesn't, use the leash to coax him gently.

9 As the dog approaches you, take hold of the toy and start a gentle tug game, letting the dog win as his reward for bringing you the toy. Repeat the exercise, but this time, you win the toy by taking it from him. Say 'leave' and put the toy away. This will end the exercise on a positive note and leave the dog wanting that toy, so he will be eager to play the game next time. After this, play with that particular toy only when you have time to play fetch again.

Tug of war

Introduce the toy to the dog by offering it to him; if he takes hold of his end, have a gentle tug of war. Initially, keep the tug games short so the dog doesn't get bored; stop the game with him still wanting to continue, so that the next time you play he will be eager to join in.

After a short game, take the toy from the dog, giving a 'leave' command; reward him with a treat and/or praise when he releases it. You can stop giving the dog food treats once he gets the hang of what he is supposed to do, since the expectation of the next play session will be reward enough.

Fetch

Now that the dog is interested in the toy, the next step is to train him to bring an item back to you.

Give

Once your dog has learnt to fetch, the next step is to teach him to release the toy into your hand. To control the situation and the distance the dog can travel, put him on a leash for this exercise.

Let go!

If your dog won't let go of the toy, here's how you can make him release it.

1 Be calm and quiet but determined.

2 Using the leash, coax him to you. Then ask him to sit; it is always easier to deal with a dog that is sitting rather than one jumping around.

3 Take hold of the toy but do not pull it; place the thumb and forefinger of your free hand under the dog's muzzle. Apply gentle pressure to his jowls, pushing them up and over his bottom teeth. At the same time give the command 'give'. The dog will then release his grip and you will be able to take the toy. The intention, of course, is not to hurt the dog, but just to make him a bit uncomfortable until he releases the toy.

After repeating this exercise two or three times you will find that as soon as you put your finger and thumb under the dog's jaw, he will respond to your command. In the future, you will be able to call the dog into the sit position in front of you, reach for the toy and say 'give', and the dog will release it into your hand.

Key points

- Make the games short and pleasant. Your dog will quickly lose interest in a toy if the game is boring.

- Alternate winners when you play tug games or the dog will not want to play when he realizes that he will never win the prize.

- When playing tug games with your dog, move the toy sideways, not up and down, to avoid damaging his neck or spine.

- Never force your dog to release an item by shouting at him, or smacking him, or by grabbing and pulling at the 'prize'. This may make the dog aggressive and possessive of his toys because it reinforces the notion that the item is important and should be jealously guarded.

- Do not expect the dog to understand the exercise immediately. He is used to playing with his toys, not retrieving them and giving them to you.

9 Recall

Once your dog knows his name, you need to train him to come back to you (recall) the instant you call him. This is essential for safety when he is off-leash and running free.

If the dog knows that coming back to you means he will be rewarded, he is more likely to comply. Initially, the reward should be of high value, such as a really tasty treat or a prized toy, but as your dog becomes conditioned to return to you on command, praise will probably be sufficient. You can, however, give occasional high-value rewards to maintain immediate response.

Put him to the test

When your dog is obediently coming back to you the first time you call, try the recall exercise in a group of one or two quiet dogs you both know, first on a long leash for control, and in case you need to reinforce the exercise from the beginning.

Approach the other (leashed) dogs with your dog on an extended leash. Before they meet and greet, call him back to you by saying his name and then 'come' or 'here'. If your dog comes to you, praise him lavishly and give him a treat or toy. If not, simply reel the leash in and drop to one knee as he nears, encouraging him to come to you and rewarding him as he reaches you. Then try again.

Once your dog is recalling well in this situation, try him off-leash, but go back a step to using the leash if you are unsuccessful. Eventually, try the exercise with all the dogs off-leash.

Teaching him to come to you

1 To begin, walk forward with your dog on a long leash and at heel as usual. Then allow the leash to go slack and move backwards, calling your dog's name and the command 'come' at the same time. Offer a treat or high-value toy to elicit a quick response.

Stop!

This exercise, which is similar to the recall, is used if you need to stop the dog suddenly when he is walking on the leash – for example, if you have just seen some broken glass hidden in the grass directly in front of him you will want him to stop instantly to avoid stepping on it. You can use either of the 'stop' or 'stay' commands as you prefer, but be consistent.

To begin, walk along at a normal pace with the lead in your left hand, shortened so there is not much slack, and the dog at heel. Then slow down a little to give yourself time to do the following: simultaneously give the command 'stop' and a quick tug backwards on the leash, and bring your right hand down, palm open, in a sharp chopping motion in front of the dog.

Practise speeding up this command, and reward your dog each time he responds instantly. The idea is to eliminate the need to stop the dog physically with the leash, as the dog learns to respond to your voice and hand signal alone.

2 As the dog reaches you, say 'sit', and when he responds give the treat or play a game with a toy and praise him lavishly. Once the dog is responding instantly each time you do this exercise, try dropping the leash on the ground (within easy reach in case you need to grab it) to see what his reaction is. When you are happy with the dog's response, try the exercise off-leash in a secure area, gradually increasing the distance between you.

TRAINER'S TIP

Take this exercise slowly: you do not want to move too fast, too soon and have to keep going back to the beginning. Eventually this will have a negative effect, and the dog will start to ignore your recall command.

Sit-stay

The natural progression from the stop exercise is the sit-stay, first with the dog on a long leash, then off-leash.

To begin, have the dog ahead of you on the long leash. Call his name to get his attention, then step towards him (rather than have him come back to you) with your hand up, palm facing the dog, and command 'sit-stay'. When he does, walk up to him and give him a reward. Then try it again, but this time call the dog to you after the sit-stay, and reward him on his return.

Alternate walking to and calling the dog so he does not become accustomed to the same exercise but will stop, sit and stay on command both on and off the leash, waiting for you either to go up to him or command him to come to you.

Off-leash emergency stop

Occasionally, when you are out on a walk with your dog off-leash, you may encounter a situation where you suddenly need to stop your dog in his tracks and have him return to you. You can effect such an emergency stop by using either a rattle pot or a dog training whistle.

Key points

- Be sure to train the recall and stop exercises in a safe, enclosed area and not a local park, which is neither.

- The dog must respond to the recall before you move on to the stop exercise.

- If problems arise, go back a couple of steps and reinforce these before going on. If you still have difficulties, consult a professional trainer. It is very important that your dog recalls when you want him to do so.

- Practise the recall and stop regularly, but in short sessions.

- Always finish on a success. If the dog recalls or stops the first time, end the lesson there, leaving him with a positive association.

Emergency stop

1 Use a rattle pot – a tin or plastic container half-filled with small pebbles with a tight lid and should be small enough to fit into a pocket. Shake the pot to catch the dog's attention. Immediately call his name and offer an irresistible treat.

2 Instead of a rattle pot, you can use a dog training whistle. Keep it on a chain around your neck when you are out with your dog so you have immediate access to it if necessary.

3 If the dog takes off after something, give a sharp blast on the whistle. This should make him stop and look back to see where the sudden noise has come from.

4 The instant your dog looks back, call him to you and reward him lavishly when he returns.

10 Social skills

A dog who is well socialized with humans and other animals is less likely to develop behaviour problems. Dogs generally love the company of humans and their own kind, so it's important to socialize your dog so both of you can lead more fulfilled and stress-free lives. The principles of socializing puppies also apply to adult dogs (see pages 42–43).

If you have an adult dog who hasn't been socialized properly – that is, he has not had the chance to meet many people or other dogs – you need to address this situation carefully and correctly. The best way to do this is to find a good training school that holds socialization classes for older dogs in a controlled, safe environment. Doing this will make you feel more confident, too, especially if you have a dog who gets over-excited or even becomes aggressive when he meets people or other dogs, and you are not sure how to cope with the situation.

The ideal is to have a dog who you know is there, but who doesn't let you know he is there. Teaching your dog to sit quietly when visitors call makes life more pleasant for all concerned.

Introductions

Having a dog who will sit and stay on command is the key to successful introduction, integration and interaction. If you can control your dog calmly, you stand a better chance of having him accept the situations around him so that interacting with other people and animals is more likely to be a positive experience for both of you.

When starting to socialize your dog, remember that you cannot force him to accept friends; he has to do that at his own pace. What you can do

is help him simply by staying calm yourself. If he feels the leash begin to tighten, he will get the impression that you are not happy with the situation, and he will react in kind. Try to let the leash stay a little bit slack, although not too loose. If you give him too much room to move about, he may panic.

- Do not force your dog to socialize; give him time and the opportunity to accept others at his own pace. Forcing him may result in an aggressive or nervous dog.

- Avoid over-enthusiastic offers of help and advice that may push the dog in the wrong direction.

- Do not be afraid to seek professional help from a trainer. Socialization is an important aspect of your dog's emotional make-up.

- Make visitors aware of your rules regarding the dog, such as not giving him attention the minute they walk in to avoid elevating his status and encouraging him to seek attention.

- For the safety of both parties, do not let children play with a dog unsupervised.

A dog who is willing to play is a happy dog.
Taking your dog to classes where he can socialize
with others will bring out the best in him.

It is important that children – and even
adult visitors, for that matter – know not
to take liberties with your dog such as
grabbing at his tail or paws in play, or
encouraging him to play-bite at arms
or clothing.

Appropriate playing

There is a tendency for children to
rush straight up to any dog they see
and put their hands all over him or
even give him a hug. This is a
potentially frightening experience for
the dog, as he does not know that the
child's intentions are non-threatening.
He may view the action as aggressive
and snap to protect himself.

It is important to keep an eye on
children when they are playing with a
dog. They can get carried away and
not realize when a game is getting
out of hand, with the dog becoming
over-excited and therefore liable to
play rough.

Discourage children from playing
tug games with your dog because
they may not know when to stop. The
dog could become reluctant to
relinquish the tug, and become
aggressive towards the child.

Human hands

If you have a chance to meet people you know in
the park it's fine, but do not try to push your dog
into meeting others. Do not let your friends
approach the dog and reach straight down to
touch him; instead, ask them to ignore him
initially and perhaps drop a treat or two in front of
him. You will be surprised at how quickly he will
want to investigate a hand that is dropping treats!

The point of this exercise is that the dog
approaches the hand and not the other way
around, so he sees hands as being good. The
reason for this tactic is this: you may not know
the history of the dog, especially if he is from a
rescue centre. If he was physically abused in the
past, he may well be hand-shy and either duck
away from an approaching hand or snap at it as
a defensive measure.

11 House manners

It is important for your dog to understand his place in the household and behave appropriately. For example, you should be able to greet visitors at the door without your dog rushing to get there first or refusing to let them in. It's not his job to greet them; it's your place as pack leader to do that. If your dog does not understand this, you may find that after a while, people stop visiting and you may even start to lose friends. If this is the case, your dog is doing you no favours; likewise, by not training him to socialize properly, you are being unfair to your dog.

Take the lead

There are a number of things you can do to implement house rules that your dog understands. When you come home at any time of day, do what you need to do first, such as taking off your coat off and hanging it up or putting the groceries away. Do anything at all *except* go straight to the dog and give him attention.

While the dog is rushing around in excitement at your return and demanding attention, ignore him. You don't want to reinforce his notion that he has high status in the household and should be deferred to. After two or three minutes he will become fed up with being ignored and will either find something to do or lie down. At this point, call him and give him a few minutes of attention.

Explain this strategy to your guests, and if they agree to go along with it, let the dog be in the same room. Ask your friends to sit down and ignore the dog. If he tries to get up on a guest's lap or chair, gently but firmly push him down without saying anything to him. Even a reprimand would fulfil his desire for attention. After a few minutes, he will go away.

Leave him for a few minutes and then call him to you, using his name and the command 'come'. Give him attention for a few minutes, then gently push him away with the command 'finish', and remove your arms and hands from his reach.

By introducing these few firm rules, you will soon see a change in the dog's behaviour. He will not always be demanding your attention or be under your feet. When in the house, you have the right to sit and read, relax or work: it is simply bad manners for the dog to put himself in your way or refuse to move.

TRAINER'S TIP

Remember to be consistent with house rules so that the dog does not become confused; not allowing him to do something one day and then allowing it the next may result in the formation of stress/anxiety induced behaviours.

Enforce house rules

Here is a typical example of a dog with no house manners: you need to go from one room to another, but as you get up, the dog also gets up and stands or lies in the doorway, blocking your exit. You end up either trying to move him out of the way or stepping over him. This is a mistake, as you are deferring to the dog and thereby elevating his status. So how do you get your dog to understand what you want? Remember, if he doesn't understand, he can't possibly comply.

With a dog who insists on sitting or standing in the doorway as you are trying to pass through, you should first try to pre-empt the behaviour and deal with it before it becomes a problem. As you are getting up from your seat, give the dog a 'stay' command, which tells him what you want him to do. Provided you have taught the dog what this means, he will obey. If you haven't taught him to stay he cannot comply because he doesn't know what you mean. (Teaching a dog to stay is described on pages 66–67.)

If the dog is already standing or lying in the doorway, tell him to move using the 'away' command; do *not* step over him. (Teaching 'away' is described on pages 68–69.)

As you try to exit the room you find your dog lying in front of the doorway.

Use the 'away' command rather than simply stepping over him.

How to stop attention-seeking behaviour

GOLDEN RULES

Remember these three golden rules:

• You pay the bills therefore you are the pack leader.

• Your dog is just that – a dog. He does not contribute to providing food, warmth and shelter for the pack.

• This means that you are Number One in the pecking order, and your dog is at the bottom.

1 If your dog demands your attention by jumping up and pawing at your legs while you are doing something else, such as trying to read, you should ignore him.

2 When he gets no reaction from you, he will sit down and consider the situation.

3 The dog will lie down quietly while deciding what his next move should be.

4 Soon after he lies down, it is important that you reward this desired behaviour. This way, the dog will associate non-attention-seeking behaviour with a pleasant, positive experience, and learn that leaping around trying to get attention brings no reward at all.

Rules for feeding

When you are teaching your dog manners, setting rules for feeding is essential. In the wild, a pack of dogs has a leader who provides food for them; the leader also eats first. You should imitate this behaviour in your home by making it clear that you and your family eat before the dog is allowed his food. Try the following exercise.

1 Place the dog's food bowl on the table while you prepare his meal. Make him sit quietly while you do this.

2 Place a plate of biscuits behind the bowl.

3 Get each family member to take a biscuit and eat it while the dog watches; it will appear to him that you are eating from his bowl.

4 After you have done this, leave the dog for a few minutes, then come back and put his food on the floor, saying 'leave' as you do. Wait until the dog looks at you for permission, then let him eat.

Through this exercise, the order of the pack hierarchy is reinforced: the human family members head the list, with the dog at the bottom.

WEEKEND CORRECTIVE TRAINING:
cure the 12 most common problems

Training Plan

Weekend 1:

- To combat separation anxiety, gradually reduce the dog's dependence on you and implement an appropriate socialization programme (see pages 80–81).

- Restrict him to certain areas of the house that are easy to clean in case of soiling. Begin toilet training. Implement a feeding routine where he may go outside shortly after eating.

- Do not leave him for prolonged periods where he is unable to relieve himself.

- Provide activity toys to occupy him when he is left alone.

- Restrict access to furniture that the dog likes to sit on and begin 'climbing on furniture' training (see pages 114–115).

- Begin training to prevent pulling on the leash (see pages 100–101)

- Go back to basics with house manners (see pages 82–85) and food training (see pages 52–53) to demote his status within the family 'pack'.

Weekend 2:

- After a week of the corrective training outlined in week one, coupled with continual reinforcement, you should be seeing a difference in all problem areas. Continue with all areas of training as necessary.

- If you have not already done so, put a command to urinating and defecating.

Weekend 3:

- By now, providing you have implemented a care and training routine that works for you and your dog, it is likely that if all problem areas have not been cured already, you are three-quarters of the way there in solving them.

Weekend 4:

- If you are having real problems, then it would be a good idea to seriously consider getting professional help, so consult a reputable trainer – your vet may be able to recommend someone.

Why does my dog misbehave? This is a question that dog trainers hear all the time. But think about it: is your dog really misbehaving, or is he doing what *he* thinks is the right thing?

There are a number of reasons why dogs behave as they do. Usually, it's because they have been forced into it by human interference. In a wild pack, dogs interact naturally with one another and with other animals. They quickly learn about the pecking order and social skills within the pack, as well as exactly where they fit into it.

How long does corrective training take?

You have a good chance of solving an area of problem behaviour in one weekend, provided you follow up the initial training with continual reinforcement to stay on top of the problem and re-focus the dog on what type of behaviour is rewarding for him.

Where a dog has two or more habits that you would like to remove, then you can work on them simultaneously. To work out a training programme, assess your dog's needs and read the detailed instructions on areas of corrective training in the following pages. Then break down the training needs into progressive sections.

The chart (left) is a sample training schedule for a fit and healthy dog who pulls on the leash, jumps on furniture and soils in the house.

The first step is to ascertain why the dog is behaving in this way. He could have a physical problem, so get him checked by a vet. Did something happen that triggered the behaviours? Keep a diary of when the problems occur. Provided that the vet gives the dog a clean bill of health, reasons for the dog's behaviours may include:

• Separation anxiety. Some dogs display such behaviours when left on their own.
• A lack of basic training.
• A lack of basic care, for example the dog does not have access to outside to relieve himself. He may not be getting enough exercise, and is so keen to go for walks that he pulls on the leash.

Depending on the circumstances and progress made from one week to the next, along with the time you can devote to caring for your dog's needs, the desired result of a lead-obedient, house-trained and mannerly dog may arrive sooner or take longer than the four-week programme suggested here. Refer to the relevant detailed information given in the following sections for training instructions.

The human factor

With domesticated dogs, the human element comes into the equation and upsets the natural status quo. A dog enters a household as a puppy quite willing to learn from the pack leaders, but unfortunately (in many cases), the human pack leader who should be setting the examples and rules throws them straight out of the window because 'the puppy looked at me with those lovely brown eyes'.

TRAINING TIP

There is often no quick-fix solution where some behavioural problems are concerned, such as aggression, chasing other animals and car travel problems, so you have to be prepared for a prolonged and sustained programme of re-training.

Guilt trip

Human beings believe that because they look and feel guilty about doing something wrong, so does a dog. However, this is not necessarily the way a dog sees things. A prime example is a dog who has soiled in the house. Since this is a natural function for a dog, why should he feel guilty?

The dog's timid appearance when you come home to the dirty floor is probably not due to his guilt at having soiled but to your angry tone of voice and hostile body language. Instead of being annoyed with the dog, you should be cross with yourself. Aim to solve the 'problem' by asking yourself how it could have been prevented.

How old is the dog? Could he reasonably be expected to last the length of time you were gone without needing to relieve himself? More importantly, ask yourself if you have toilet-trained your dog correctly so that he knows where to go. (For details on toilet training and dealing with soiling in the house, see pages 46–47 and 102–103.)

As soon as you give in to the first whim of the puppy or adult dog, you are on the way to having a pet whom you see as misbehaving. The dog sees this as his chance to become the leader of the pack in his own environment.

The following pages demonstrate how you can correct problems that have developed or have come with a dog you have adopted. The key to all successful corrective training is not to be angry at the dog, which won't achieve anything positive; instead, show him an alternative that is more rewarding for everyone. And you can make huge progress in just a weekend!

TRAINER'S TIP

A dog that guards his food or toys is a liability. Sooner or later, someone is likely to be bitten. Teaching your dog not to be possessive is essential right from the start (see pages 72–75).

How owners cause problems

attention-seeking

A dog playing tug with his owner will quickly realize he is the boss if he is allowed to win all the time. He should also not be allowed to dictate when you play. Instead, you should begin the game by inviting him to play. Then he must recognize when the game is over, which is when you have had enough. However, more often than not the dog continues to toss the toy onto your knee, and instead of ignoring him, you throw the toy on the floor just for a bit of peace. The dog immediately realizes that he has your attention, and the game will continue on his terms, not yours.

chewing

If you give your puppy or adult dog an old shoe or item of clothing to play with, don't be surprised to find him taking and chewing the family's clothes and shoes, because he can't differentiate between the items you no longer need and the ones you do.

sitting on furniture

A dog does not just decide that he is going to sit on the furniture. Probably at some point, he was invited up onto his owner's knee because 'he was cute and wanted a cuddle'. In the wild, these animals obviously wouldn't have furniture to sit on, so it is the owner who causes the problem in the first place.

From a dog's point of view

The human misunderstanding of the role of the pack leader leads to canine behaviour problems. At the risk of indulging in anthropomorphism (see page 15), let's take a look at this from the dog's point of view.

'Hey, I've got a new owner. I wonder if he is going to be like the last one? Owners are all the same; they want us to do things for them, but I don't know what it means when I'm off the leash in the park and my owner starts to chase me around, shouting and screaming. What does "come here" mean, anyway? Whenever my old owner shouted "come here" and caught me, he gave me a beating. Well, if this one thinks I'll fall for that again, he has another think coming.

'These people are funny creatures. They get you home and give you a smelly old slipper to play with, then when you've chewed that up and find a fresh one, they get really angry. It's only a slipper, after all, just like the one they gave you in the first place.

'They let you get up on the sofa when you're a puppy and then, just because you weigh more and slobber all over the place, they don't like it. And another thing: why is it all right to sit on your favourite chair until company comes, but then you're expected to give it up for one of them?

'I wish that people who take us in would decide what they want from us in the first place, then explain what they mean when they say something. After all, I am a dog – a pet – and I am just here to please. If only I knew how.'

rough play

If you decide to get down on the floor and play-wrestle with the dog, it's likely that he will try to dominate the situation: he will end up on top and you will be lying on the floor with the dog chewing on various parts of your body. This is the point at which you will start to get up and tell the dog to leave you alone because he has probably nipped you, and it hurts! Suddenly, you think your dog has become badly behaved or aggressive, but actually he is only doing exactly what he would do in a pack situation. You may tolerate this behaviour in a puppy, but it can become a real problem in an adult dog.

begging and stealing

If you make the mistake of feeding your dog scraps from the table because he looks hungry or he was in a rescue centre and you feel you have to make up for the poor start he had in life, you are creating a problem for yourself. You will end up with the dog helping himself from the table or counter, and encourage him to sit and salivate while you are preparing or eating your meal. He will start to beg for food, and if that doesn't work, he will sit and bark until you give him food from your plate.

1 Aggressive behaviour

Aggression in dogs is not always what it seems: sometimes, what you perceive as nastiness is in fact fear. The dog is being defensive, having learned that showing his teeth and growling usually make potential adversaries, or anyone or anything causing him discomfort, back off. Whatever the cause, it presents a serious problem for owners and is extremely difficult to overcome unless the owner is prepared to invest a great deal of time and money in re-training.

Sadly, sometimes aggression is so deeply ingrained and the dog so unpredictable that there is no option other than to have him put to sleep. However, these cases are rare, and with the right approach and commitment from the owner, it is possible to turn an apparently aggressive dog into a more affable and even-tempered companion.

Teaching non-aggressive behavior

1 An owner can unwittingly cause a dog to become aggressive towards other dogs or people. For instance, when you are out walking and your dog tries to hide behind you when a person or dog approaches, the worst thing you can do is try to reassure him. If he needs reassurance, the dog will reason, then there really must be something to be afraid of. Sensing your tension, he will snap as a defensive measure. If this works – and it usually does – and the 'adversary' backs off, your dog learns that his behaviour achieves the desired result. Unfortunately, you then perceive the dog to have an aggressive attitude towards other dogs and people.

2 Instead of reacting to your dog's nervousness with other people or dogs, simply ignore him and continue what you are doing. This in itself will reassure your dog that there is nothing to be frightened of and he has no need to be defensive.

TRAINER'S TIP

Professional help is a must when dealing with aggression in any form. Find a good dog trainer who can help and advise you on the most appropriate re-training for your dog. Trainers see this kind of behaviour all the time and know the best ways to deal with it, all the while taking into account both the owner's capabilities and lifestyle.

3 To begin, re-train your dog in situations with people and dogs whom you know so the other owners fully understand what you are trying to do and will respect the need for a controlled session and 'meet and greet' with their dogs. Let your dog investigate the other dog or person in his own time; do not force an introduction. Once he has reassured himself that there is no need to take defensive action and relaxes, you can praise him and give him a treat. This way, he learns to view other people or dogs as rewarding rather than as potential threats.

When a dog barks and appears aggressive towards passers-by while out walking, and the owner is unable to get the dog's attention despite his best efforts, it shows that the owner has very little control. If this sounds familiar, you might try using a headcollar on your dog. Not only will this give him something to think about other than terrorizing passers-by, it will also give you more control. But talk to a trainer about it first, since some items of equipment may actually make the situation worse, depending on the reason for your dog's aggression.

4 Taking your dog to socialization classes is extremely beneficial. At first, it will be an on-leash experience with other well-trained and non-aggressive dogs of a similar size (a small dog would be even more intimidated in a class of Great Danes!). Gradually you can progress to mixing with all types of dogs off-leash as yours becomes more confident in himself and therefore more sociable.

5 Agility classes are great for socialization. The dogs are usually too busy enjoying themselves to think of viewing their classmates as adversaries, and by the time the session is over, they have discovered that it is much more rewarding to play together than to fight.

Without a headcollar, your dog is easily able to look at a passer-by and bark to his heart's content.

With a headcollar, you can gently turn your dog's head so he has to look away from the passer-by.

Case history: nervous aggression

The dog • While working a class at a rescue centre, Keith Davis was approached by Rhonda and Jack. With them was a little dog with his tail curled between his legs and his ears folded down. He could not have tucked himself any further into the back of Rhonda's legs if he had tried. He was truly terrified. The dog, named Billy, was 4½ years old and had been adopted from a rescue centre.

The problem • As Rhonda explained, Billy was aggressive to people who passed by or stopped to talk to them and also towards dogs that he saw – and if they dared to come near her, he went crazy. When Keith approached Billy, his response was a bark and a growl to show his full set of teeth.

The solution • Keith told Rhonda and Jack to take Billy away from everyone else and just to sit and watch the class at work. Keith then worked the class closer and closer to where the three were sitting. Introducing treats in order to distract Billy proved very helpful, and soon he was watching and listening to Rhonda, who spoke to him every time a dog or owner came near. When Billy responded to her voice, he was rewarded.

This initial work continued for a couple of sessions, then progressed to Rhonda and Billy walking around the training area, but ignoring what everyone else was doing in class. The next step was to include Billy in the group for the socializing exercises and, with Rhonda using the same method of treat distraction, he soon began to ignore people and dogs who walked past at a distance. Gradually his classmates came closer and closer, until eventually another dog was able to sit next to Billy without any adverse reaction from him.

Over a period of time, Billy was allowed off-leash for short periods to check his response (the other dogs in that class were well-trained and kept on-leash). He was initially very reluctant to leave Rhonda, but over several weeks he gradually began to investigate the perimeter of the training area and was willing to approach a couple of the quieter dogs.

At this point, Keith encouraged other handlers to talk to but not touch Billy and to offer him treats, which he took. Suddenly he seemed much more confident in his surroundings. He would even allow Keith to stroke him, although only while he was standing with Rhonda and Jack.

While Billy would never be the most confident dog in the world, he was now quite happy to walk around without becoming a nervous wreck if someone looked at him. Rhonda was overjoyed; because of the training sessions, she could at least take Billy for a run in the park and, more importantly, she knew he was enjoying life a whole lot more.

When dogs bite

If the problem has become so severe that your dog actually bites, or you are sure that it is only a matter of time until he does, it is essential to seek help from a professional trainer, especially if there are children in the house. You cannot hope to deal effectively with the problem yourself.

In the meantime, do not walk your dog – and certainly don't let him off the leash in public places – without a muzzle. Actually, it's safer not to exercise him in public places at all, since with a muzzle on he would not be able to defend himself if another dog attacked him.

TRAINER'S TIP

The minute you think there may be a problem with aggression in your dog, no matter how slight, seek professional help from a trainer. This way you are likely to prevent any serious problems developing.

Fitting a muzzle

 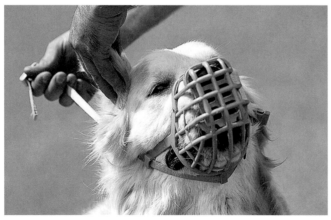 

1 When using a muzzle you must be sure it fits correctly, or your dog will be uncomfortable, which will only increase his aggression. If you are unsure about the best muzzle to use, ask a trainer, then be sure it is the correct size and fit for the dog. To put a muzzle on, first slip it gently over the dog's nose.

2 Put the headpiece behind the dog's head, carefully lifting his ears out of the way so they don't get trapped.

3 Fasten the headpiece, making sure it isn't too tight by sliding the flat of your hand between it and the dog's neck. Conversely, if it is not tight enough, the dog will be able to dislodge it easily.

Key points ✓

- With any form of canine aggression, seek immediate advice and practical help from an experienced trainer. Don't try dealing with the problem on your own; it won't work.

- Do not let your dog gain the upper hand at home. Pay particular attention to food training, socializing and house manners (see pages 52–53 and 80–85).

- Take your dog for a veterinary examination, to see if the aggression is due to an underlying physical problem that is causing discomfort and making him irritable.

- Your demeanour and actions towards your dog have a huge effect on his temperament. A stressed-out, irritable owner tends to pass on his tension to his dog, resulting in a nervous, defensive animal who is likely to develop into an aggressive one.

- The importance of socializing your dog cannot be over-emphasized: go to training classes at least once a week and you will gradually see a difference in any but the most emotionally disabled dog.

Case history: jealous aggression

The dog • Bob, a five-year-old Golden Retriever, belonged to Margaret and John, a retired couple. They got him as a pup and he had spent all his time with John, going everywhere with him. But then it got to the point where Bob had taken over, deciding who could come into the house and what people could and couldn't do inside the home. He became aggressive towards visitors and began to threaten other family members.

The problem • When the couple started to look after their three-year-old grandson during the day, Bob became jealous of the attention the toddler was getting and had actually mouthed the child's body. Understandably, the little boy's parents refused to let him return to his grandparents' home until the dog had been either dealt with or destroyed.

The solution • Keith Davis visited the home without the child being present, and as he walked in, he encountered warning signs of aggression from Bob. It was apparent to Keith that Bob had decided that he was now top dog and therefore in charge of the household. Keith advised the owners of a suitable re-training routine that would, over a period of time, reinstate them as pack leaders. This involved the couple ignoring Bob until he had settled down and not playing with him or fussing over him if he demanded attention. In addition, they were told to teach Bob to leave the room on command and to sit or lie quietly and stay where he was told until they called him to them.

Over a number of weeks, Bob was taught that it was all right to bark when people knocked at the door, but then, on command, he had to go and lie down quietly and not greet visitors until requested to do so. Keith also advised Bob's owners to change their feeding routine so it placed the dog at the bottom of the pack by giving Bob his meal only when they had finished theirs. In addition, he was not to be allowed into the room in which they were eating.

Eventually, the grandchild was introduced back into the equation: the plan was to make Bob understand that the little boy was a higher-ranking pack member, not a lower one and therefore a threat to his perceived position as top dog. Under adult supervision, this was implemented by the child eating first, then giving Bob a treat so the dog viewed him as a source of pleasure and reward.

Bob soon adapted very well to his lowest-ranking position in the family pack, and all the human members of the family were pleased with the results of the corrective training.

2 Barking

Barking is a dog's way of speaking and is used to sound an alarm and warn other pack members of intruders, as an effective way of warning off potential foes and also to indicate a state of high excitement, such as during play.

While barking can be a positive canine reaction in appropriate situations – during play, or to deter intruders at home or would-be attackers while out walking – it can be negative when the dog barks inappropriately. Examples include barking every time someone walks by outside the house or continuing to bark at the door long after he has announced that a visitor has arrived.

TRAINER'S TIP

Some breeds are more vocal than others, so bear this in mind when choosing a dog – especially if you live in a highly populated area.

How do I deal with barking?

To deal with inappropriate barking, you must teach the dog that such vocal behaviour is unrewarding and that quiet behaviour is more rewarding. Simply telling the dog to be quiet on its own won't work because there is no incentive for him to obey. In fact, barking is rewarding to the dog because you are paying attention to him, so he will continue. In the dog's mind, any attention, even being told off, is better than none at all.

However, if you follow the command 'quiet' with a reward when the dog responds, he will quickly learn that 'quiet' means a reward if he stops barking.

Achieving a conditioned response

You have to be consistent when re-training and keep reinforcing what the dog has learned until the response is almost automatic. This is known as a conditioned response. Teaching a dog to do something and then not reinforcing the lessons doesn't work. To maintain a desired behaviour, a dog needs 'refreshers' every day.

Apply this to re-training a barking dog. Say that you've trained your dog to be quiet on command but then on a couple of occasions, he barks when someone comes to the door and you don't correct him. The next time someone comes to the door, you do use the 'quiet' command, but the dog ignores you. Now you have to go back several steps to start the training again.

Training him not to bark

1 When your dog barks for attention, ignore him until he settles down and is quiet. Avoid eye contact and fold your arms out of his reach.

2 When the dog realizes that you aren't responding to his barking, he will settle down to see what happens next. When he does, use the command 'quiet' and reward him with a treat, praise and attention. Once he has grasped the association between 'quiet' and a reward, he will start to obey. After this, praise and attention will be enough to maintain the response.

3 Another option is to take the dog out of the room when he barks inappropriately and let him back in only when he is quiet. When you let him in, use the command 'quiet'. If he barks, take him out again. He will soon learn that barking is unrewarding (he is banished from the room) while being quiet is rewarding (he is allowed to re-join his pack).

Noise nuisance

People often complain that their dogs bark in the house or garden when they are out all day. Why is this?

1 The main reason is that left to his own devices, without companionship, the dog is quite simply bored and is looking for a way to amuse himself, and barking at passers-by fulfils that need.

2 Another reason is that the dog has taken on the responsibility of guarding the family home in your absence and is warning off potential intruders.

3 The third reason, particularly if the dog howls rather than barks, is that he is calling to his pack to come home.

Depending on the reason for the behaviour, you have various options for dealing with it.

• Have someone come in at least once during your absence to let the dog out and give him some exercise and attention. This will break up his day and reduce the time he has to wait for someone to come home.

• Supply your dog with a selection of activity toys to keep him occupied. These could include puzzle feeders filled with biscuits and a couple of stuffed Kongs, but be sure to deduct the amount of food that you give him in this way from his daily ration.

• Don't leave the dog in the garden, where he is more likely to react to passers-by and other activity he can see. If for some reason you don't want to leave him in the house, take him to a dog-sitter while you are out. This costs money, but the welfare of your dog is your responsibility, and you have a duty to your neighbours to see that your dog doesn't disturb them.

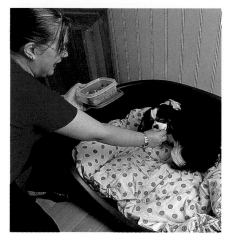

4 You can also teach your dog to go to his bed, or other designated area of the house, and stay there quietly when he hears or sees something that would normally make him bark. Do this by telling him 'bed' or 'place', and giving him some treats from a container when someone comes to the door or walks past the house. (Ask a friend to help you with this by ringing the doorbell, knocking on the door or walking past the window.) The dog's focus will be on the treat rather than on barking.

5 Put the container next to the 'quiet spot' so the dog can see it but not reach it. Reward him again if he is quiet and remains there. He will then regard this as a nice place to go to and be quiet, rather than bark. If you keep reinforcing this treat training, you should soon start to see a positive result.

Key points

- To prevent inappropriate barking, you must show the dog that an alternative behaviour is more rewarding.

- If you are going to be out all day and you know your dog is likely to bark, take steps so that he isn't left alone to suffer separation anxiety or boredom. Employ a dog-sitter, take him to a kennel and/or provide him with toys to keep him occupied.

- Enlist the help of a friend who can come to the door and knock or ring the bell so you can practise the training methods described.

- Keep the training sessions short so that the dog doesn't become bored or immune to the training method, and always end on a positive note. If the dog responds instantly to a training method, end the session. Practise again the following day to reinforce what he has learned.

- Use the training techniques whenever your dog barks inappropriately. Ignoring the training a few times may make your dog think it is fine to bark again and you could find it more difficult to break the habit this time.

Using a spray collar

In cases where the dog is an habitual barker and all other suggested control options have failed, it is worth considering using a spray collar. This collar is sound activated: when the dog barks, the collar emits a non-painful but alarming spray of liquid (usually citronella-scented) under the dog's chin. He soon learns that not barking is much more rewarding: no barking, no sudden gush of smelly liquid under his chin.

There is also a remote control version of this collar so you can determine when to activate the spray, but you must do it the instant that inappropriate barking occurs, or the exercise will be pointless and confusing for the dog.

Case history: a confirmed barker

The dog • Toby, a three-year-old Rottweiler.

The problem • Toby barked through the window at passers-by and at visitors to the house, and if he was put into another room, he would bark to be let back in.

The solution • Keith Davis paid Toby a home visit. The dog barked at the door and bounced around him as he entered. John, the owner, pulled Toby away, told him what a good boy he was, and shut him in another room. Keith deduced that Toby had assumed the role of pack leader in the house, with the responsibility for allowing visitors in and people to pass by outside. During the time Keith took to explain this to John, Toby stopped barking. He had never been left that long before.

Keith went outside, then re-entered the house. This time John ignored Toby. Keith also ignored Toby. Within a few minutes, he stopped jumping up and barking.

Next, Keith sat down and turned his body away from Toby as he conversed with John. Within a few minutes, Toby stopped barking; he paced back and forth between Keith and John, looking for guidance and explanation. After a few more minutes, he wandered off and lay down.

The next stage was to tell Toby what was expected of him. Keith stood up and moved around, but instead of letting the dog do what he thought should be done, John told him 'quiet' and 'stay'. Toby did as he was told.

Keith advised John on how to break Toby's barking habit. The most important thing was that anyone coming to to the house should ignore Toby until he had settled down.

A couple of weeks later, Keith went back to see how John was doing. When he entered the house, Toby barked a couple of times but did not jump up. Then, not getting any response from either person, he quietly sat down. The dog's behaviour at the window when people passed by had also improved and was continuing to do so.

3 Pulling on the leash

Curing a dog who pulls while you are walking him on the leash is quite simple when you know how. If the dog begins to move in front of you or starts to pull, stand still, put gentle tension on the leash and wait for the dog to come back to your side. Then praise him, command him to 'heel' and begin walking again.

As an experiment, try walking around the garden with your dog off the leash; use the heel command and your left hand to coax the dog to you. If this works, repeat the command, but this time put a treat in your left hand. Walk only five or ten paces, then reward the dog.

Keep the treats in your left-hand pocket. Your dog will soon learn they are there, so he will pay better attention to you and respond to your commands. Gradually increase the distance you walk between rewards.

You should find that this reinforcement of the 'heel' command works quickly to stop your dog pulling.

The element of surprise

1 If your dog pulls, don't pull back since it will simply encourage him to strain harder at the leash. Instead, stop and walk backwards. Surprised, the dog will stop and look to you for direction. Re-position him at your side with the command 'heel' and resume walking. Repeat this exercise whenever necessary, and the dog will soon realize that pulling is unrewarding and walking to heel is a much more relaxed experience.

2 Vary your pace while out walking: jog, change direction, stop and then walk on again. If your dog cannot predict what you are going to do next, he will keep his attention on you rather than charging full steam ahead to what he thinks is his destination.

Key points

- It is important to select the correct equipment and then fit and use it properly: get advice from a trainer. Equipment alone will not cure a problem; you have to implement training procedures, too (see pages 58–61).

- Reinforce your position as pack leader at all times, in the house as well as outside. Dogs will often pull if they think they are in charge.

- Do not let your dog stop and sniff the ground when walking, or he will soon train you to stop and start when he wants.

Using an anti-pull harness

1 If your dog is a strong puller, you may find an anti-pull harness helpful when you re-train him to walk at heel.

2 To fit the harness, gently place it over the dog's head.

3 Carefully draw his legs through the 'armholes'.

4 Check that the harness is not too tight and that no hair and/or folds of skin are uncomfortably trapped.

5 The harness will help you achieve more control, but don't jerk hard. If you hurt the dog, he may start pulling again in an effort to escape the discomfort. You must also check regularly to be sure the harness is not chafing under the dog's legs or chest.

Case history: a quick fix

The dog • Blue, a two-year-old Labrador, was an extremely happy and energetic dog. He had been with his owner, Brenda, for ten months.

The problem • Blue was a big boy, and he pulled like a train when on the leash.

The solution • Keith Davis found that Blue's flat leather collar was too small and his leash too short: Blue couldn't move more than 30cm (12in) from Brenda's side without pulling.

Keith exchanged Blue's collar and leash for a headcollar, plus a half-check collar and a leash of the right length, then took the dog for a walk. He used the pressure of just one finger and thumb on the leash and the gentle rattle of the chain to maintain the dog's attention. Then Brenda had a go and, after learning how to use the new equipment, found she no longer had a problem. Brenda reported a week later that Blue was now a pleasure to take for walks.

4 Soiling in the house

Dog owners tend to get very annoyed when their pets soil in the house. This is understandable, but it's important to know why a dog does it. The most common reason is that he has not been toilet trained correctly. What is appropriate for puppies applies to older dogs as well. For advice on toilet training, see pages 46–47.

Persistence and timing

Some dogs dislike going out when the weather is cold or wet, preferring to relieve themselves in the comfort of their own home if they get the chance. If this is the case with your pet, be patient and, above all, persistent! Your dog will eventually get the idea that the sooner he goes, the sooner he will be back inside where it is warm and dry. Be sure to praise and reward the dog immediately so he views going outside as a positive and rewarding experience.

Pick the right times to take your dog out. If he is not ready to go, there is nothing you can do to hurry nature. Get to know his habits by noticing how long it takes after he has eaten before he needs to relieve himself, because those are the obvious times to take him out. You may have to change your dog's feeding times so they fit your daily routine, or change your own schedule.

If your dog has an accident in the house, don't scold him. It will have no positive effect and will only confuse and frighten him. Simply clean up the mess, then clean the area thoroughly with a product designed to remove lingering odours that would attract your dog back to the same spot. Ordinary household cleaners are not effective.

Take your dog outside shortly after he has eaten, since this is usually when he will need to relieve himself. At first, be prepared to wait a while for him to go, but when he does, praise and reward him lavishly. Try to encourage him to use to the same spot each time, so he associates that area with relieving himself. This will not only reinforce the behaviour, it will also make cleaning up easier if you know where to look!

TRAINER'S TIP

If practical, put your dog's food and water bowls near where he has soiled inside, so he will not return to the same spot. Generally, dogs do not eliminate near their eating, drinking and sleeping areas.

Key points

- Be prepared for toilet training to take time. To lessen the damage to your house until your dog is trained, use see-through gates to restrict him to an area where it won't matter if he has an accident.

- Some dogs will let you know when they have to go out. They may be restless, whine, or go and stand by the door. Don't ignore these signals; take your dog outside right away.

- Never get cross with a dog for having an accident. The stress of having his owner angry with him may make his behaviour worse.

- Arrange your dog's mealtimes to fit your schedule, or vice versa, so your pet has access to his designated bathroom area when required. Dogs usually need to go shortly after eating.

- You can train your dog to perform on command. To do this, use word association: as soon as your dog goes, say a word or phrase such as 'go' or 'hurry up' and then praise him. It won't be long before he learns that responding to the command earns him a reward.

Litter training

Some small breeds can be taught to use a litter tray, which is practical if you don't have a garden, or if you are away for long periods. Litter train in the same way that you would toilet train a puppy (see pages 46–7) with the litter tray taking the place of the outside location.

Choose a large, shallow-sided tray (but not so shallow that the litter spills out) and line it with old newspaper or, preferably, a brand of cat litter that absorbs liquid and odour. Some pet stores also carry litter supplies made specifically for dogs.

Clean out the tray each time your dog uses it. Either double-bag the waste and put it in the dustbin, or bag it and place it in a special receptacle for dog waste if there is one nearby (use biodegradable plastic or paper bags).

When the tray gets too smelly or dirty, rinse it with warm water and a dash of non-toxic disinfectant, then leave it to dry before refilling with clean paper or litter. It's important, however, not to disinfect over the dog's own odour too often, since this tells him where he should go.

5 Eating faeces

A dog's habit of eating his own and other animals' excrement is revolting to us. However, because dogs' instincts tell them that eating droppings is perfectly natural and acceptable, it is important for owners to understand why they do it and not to get annoyed. Instead, discourage the habit by replacing it with a more desirable alternative.

Aversion therapy

First you need to set the scene. This means collecting a selection of other animals' droppings to place in a specific training area. You also need a non-toxic, bitter-tasting solution designed for the purpose – available from pet stores, or you can make your own using mustard powder and water (see instructions on opposite page).

For the training to have the best chance of working, you should consult your vet or a canine nutrition expert about the most suitable diet for your dog. If his food supplies all the nutrients he needs, he won't feel the need to eat droppings to satisfy a nutritional deficiency.

Making faeces distasteful

1 Make the faeces distasteful and therefore unrewarding to the dog by spraying them liberally with the unpleasant-tasting liquid.

2 Walk your dog by the droppings, letting him investigate and taste them if he wants to. In most cases, he won't want to do it again.

Key points

- Do not get angry with your dog for eating faeces – it's only natural to him. Instead, learn how to change this habit into more acceptable behaviour by teaching the dog to come to you for a reward instead of eating droppings.

- Be patient and persistent: this type of re-training can take some time and repetition.

- Make the effort to understand canine behaviour (see pages 14–27), since this is the only way you can hope to relate to your dog and achieve a better working partnership with him.

- Overcome your aversion to other species' idiosyncrasies; just because they are different doesn't mean that they are abhorrent. If you can't cure them, learn to live with them, provided they are not harmful to anyone.

- Make sure your dog's diet contains all the nutrients he needs. Consult your vet or a qualified canine nutritionist on this point.

3 As the dog tastes the faeces, interrupt him by calling him to you and using the 'leave' command, rewarding him with a treat when he complies. The dog should now regard the droppings as unpleasant and turn his attention back to you as this is more rewarding.

4 Practise walking by the droppings, saying 'leave' and rewarding the dog when he obeys. He will soon learn that leaving faeces alone is more rewarding than eating them.

TRAINER'S TIP

Make faeces distateful by covering them with a foul-tasting solution, which most dogs won't touch, let alone eat. To make your own mustard solution you'll need an empty, well-washed washing-up liquid bottle or other squeezable dispenser. In a small bowl, dissolve four heaped teaspoons of mustard powder in a little hot water and stir to make a smooth paste. Gradually add more warm water, stirring continuously, to make about 0.5 litres (1 pint). Leave to cool, then pour the solution through a funnel into the bottle ready for use.

Nutritional needs

We may as well ask why humans eat things that are usually totally abhorrent to a dog, such as pickled onions. It's often because the person feels the need for the nutrients that the particular food provides.

Animals utilize nutrients in food differently from humans, and those that pass out in their droppings may be extremely desirable to or required by other animals whose bodies lack them. And, since animals don't necessarily view excrement in the same way we do, some creatures are not repelled by ingesting those nutrients in whatever form they present themselves, including faeces.

6 Come back!

A dog who won't come back to his owner when called is a risk to himself and others, so obedience in this respect is essential. Don't let your dog off-leash without first doing some remedial work, or you will simply reinforce the problem. Loose dogs nearby, a bitch in season, children playing or the smell of food are all common situations that will tempt your dog not to obey your recall command.

Teaching recall

1 If your dog's habit of not returning to you is deeply ingrained, you need to find ways to overcome his indifference to you. Never go after your dog when he won't come back to you. The dog will think it's a great game if you chase him, and will find it rewarding.

Key points

• Do not get angry with your dog when he won't come back to you; he is less likely to return if he knows he is going to be scolded.

• Do not blame the dog for not recalling; he can only respond as well as he has been taught.

• Do not feed your dog before a walk. If he is hungry, he is more likely to return to you for a food reward or want to go home for his meal.

• Do not call your dog back when you know he is unlikely to respond or you will reinforce his behaviour.

• Do not chase after your dog. Instead, walk or run away and/or hide from him. He will worry when he cannot see you and may think he is being left, so he will run after you. When he reaches you, command him to sit and wait, then praise him. Don't always attach the leash when he returns.

• For initial recall training, see pages 76–79. Achieving good recall is something you really have to work at.

• Dogs who do not receive sufficient daily exercise and playtime are more likely not to recall well.

Using high-value rewards

Take your dog out for exercise when he is hungry, and wear a pouch containing tiny pieces of his favourite treats. Let him sniff the treats before you let him off the leash and he won't go far away. Recall and reward him with a treat; he will soon realize that coming back to you on command is rewarding. Alternatively, use a high-value toy instead (see pages 72–75).

2 If your dog won't return to you on command, walk or run away from him. He will think you are leaving him and come running, anxious not to be left behind. When he reaches you, stop and tell him to sit. Reward him with praise when he does, then walk on briskly; he is sure to follow. Repeat the exercise often, until your dog doesn't want to take his eyes off you in case you disappear.

3 Don't let your dog think that because you are holding the leash or reach for his collar the walk is over, or he will be reluctant to recall. To avoid this, call the dog to you, tell him to sit and reward him with a treat or toy. Next, play with his neck and collar, then give a release command such as 'away' and send him off to play again. If you practise this often, your dog will learn that recall and leash don't always mean the end of playtime.

Make a game of recall by throwing your dog's favourite high-value toy for him to retrieve. You can make it more challenging by throwing the toy into long grass so that he has to search for and scent it out. Making walks more exciting so that the dog's attention remains on you to see what you are going to do next is the key to achieving and maintaining good recall.

TRAINER'S TIP

Another way to deal with the problem is to recall your dog, reward him when he comes, attach the leash and walk for about twenty paces, then realease him again. Practising this every time you take your dog out for exercise will remove the 'recall/leash/exercise over' association, making him more inclined to want to return to you.

When you do recall the dog, make sure that your voice and body language are encouraging and welcoming, or he won't be sure of a pleasant reception when he returns and may therefore be inclined to stay away in case he is about to be scolded.

Hide and seek

This is a great way of motivating your dog to return to you. The game works on the principle that the dog thinks you have disappeared and left him, so he will come to find you. The reward of seeking you out is then enhanced by a treat (initially) or another game with a high-value toy.

1 Send the dog away. This is reverse psychology, since the dog will think you don't want him and be more motivated to come back to you.

2 Once the dog is moving away from you, hide behind a tree or in bushes, but not too well at first, or he may panic and run off in the opposite direction if he can't find you quickly.

3 If the dog appears to be struggling to find you, call him. When he does find you, call him to you, praise him lavishly and give him a treat.

4 While he is distracted with the treat and relief at finding you, gently take hold of his collar and attach the leash. A word of warning, though: don't always do this right after this exercise. Instead, play something else with the dog, repeat the hide-and-seek game, or walk on a little further before the exercise session ends. Otherwise, your dog will associate the leash with the end of playtime and be reluctant to return to you.

Case history: clicker solution

The dog • A five-year-old cross-breed named Trudy.

The problem • Trudy and her owner, Liz, lived in a house that backed onto a field. When Trudy was let off the leash she wouldn't come back; she also insisted on pulling Liz to the field. Once off-leash she would race around and if she saw other people she would run at them, barking.

The solution • The first thing that trainer Keith Davis did was to check the equipment used for Trudy. Liz was using a short leash and check chain. The chain was tearing away the fur at Trudy's neck, so Keith suggested that Liz use a fabric collar and 2.5 metre (8 foot) training leash instead. Armed with some treats, a clicker and an extra 6 metre (20 foot) leash, off they went to the field.

Keith decided that Trudy would be likely to respond to clicker training (see page 63), so he went through the concept of the exercise with Liz before putting it into practice. Trudy responded quickly; she really enjoyed the treats used to condition her to the 'click', which she received each time her attention was focused on Liz. Then she was allowed a little more freedom, courtesy of the training leash; again, she responded well to the clicker. The instant she returned to Liz when called, Liz 'clicked' and rewarded her, so Trudy associated coming back instantly on command with a pleasant experience.

Following Keith's instructions, Liz worked on these exercises every day. Two weeks later, Keith decided it was time to try the recall when Trudy was off-leash. A couple of other training class members were used as distractions. Trudy was allowed to move away from Liz, but not to reach the 'victims' before she was recalled. The distance between Trudy and Liz was gradually increased, to the point where Trudy went part of the way to the people and was then commanded to return. When she did, she was rewarded.

These exercises were followed up with regular recall reinforcement in training classes, and eventually Trudy could play with other dogs and recall on a single command.

7 Chasing and rivalry

Dogs who chase after dogs, other animals or even people are a liability and leave their owners open to possible prosecution. A dog may even end up losing his life if he bites someone or is caught worrying livestock. Having evolved as pack animals who must find, catch and eat prey animals in order to survive, dogs have an instinct to chase anything that moves. Often this will be a playful 'practise-pursuit', though in some instances, a dog will actually attack.

Getting help

It is important to get professional help with this problem, certainly in the initial stages of training, since it's unlikely that you will solve it on your own. Some dogs have a very strong inborn chase drive and learning how to manage it, requires first-hand practical help from an expert.

Disc training can be particularly useful in re-training 'chasers', but you must be taught how to do it correctly, or it will be worthless. Find a trainer who is experienced in using a disc. Gradual, controlled socializing may also prove useful, provided there is no risk or stress to the other people and animals involved.

The most important factor in re-training a 'chaser' is to keep his attention firmly focused on you, and to be sure that he understands and responds to the 'heel', 'stay' and recall commands (see pages 58–61, 66–67 and 76–79). Also refer to pages 82–85 for how to teach your dog his place within your family 'pack'.

Key points

- If your dog reacts to dogs or other animals, find a good training school that offers socialization classes. Don't attempt to cure the problem on your own, since you are not likely to succeed. Training classes are a must.

- It is important for initial socialization to occur in a controlled environment; if other dogs are involved, they should be non-reactive.

- Do not let a 'chaser' off-leash in public places until re-training has been firmly established. Keep him on a long leash when re-training so that you have control at all times. Do not release the dog from the leash too soon, or you could undo weeks of work in a single moment.

- Discover what motivates your dog to maintain his attention on you; is it a toy or a treat? Use your knowledge to the best advantage.

- Do not wait until the problem is beyond curing before you seek professional help. You will do neither yourself nor the dog any favours by waiting for him 'to grow out of it'. The chances are he won't, and the problem will just get worse.

- Regular recall and socialization practice is essential, and not only at training classes.

Distracting exercise

1 If a particular toy motivates your dog, use that as the distraction, or use a piece of his favourite treat. When approaching whatever it is that sparks the chase instinct, call the dog's name, command 'heel' and 'stay', and show him the toy or treat.

2 If the dog reacts to the 'victim', simply ignore the behaviour and call your dog's name, offering him the distraction, with which you can reward him once you have passed the 'victim'. Soon the dog will realize that staying with you is far more rewarding than chasing after another animal or a person.

TRAINER'S TIP

When practising the distraction exercise, enlist the help of someone with a non-reactive dog. Using a retractable leash or a long line, gradually decrease the distance between your dog and your helper's non-reactive dog, until you are passing closely and your dog maintains his attention on you. Reward him for this.

Rivalry

Another potentially serious and certainly distressing problem that owners of two or more dogs sometimes encounter is when their dogs constantly fight. This is usually the result of an ongoing dispute over hierarchy, and it can be even more difficult to cure if the dogs are evenly matched in terms of sex, age and size.

If the dogs are not neutered, consult your vet about whether neutering one (usually the less dominant one) may help solve the problem. Sometimes it does, sometimes it doesn't.

Occasionally, if the rivalry is extremely intense, there is no alternative but to find a new home for one of the dogs.

Help to establish hierarchy between two dogs by giving one privileges before the other. With your vet's advice, choose the apparently dominant dog. Give him attention first, feed him first, clip on his leash first before a walk and so on. This way, the other dog will learn that he is further down the pecking order, and will not try to assert authority over his rival. In most cases, this will lead to a more harmonious relationship between the dogs; if it doesn't, you may wish to consult a canine behaviourist to help you solve the problem. Ask your vet for a referral.

Case history: the importance of socialization

The dog • Samson was an 18-month-old Labrador who had been owned by Lorraine since he was ten weeks old.

The problem • Although good in all other respects, Samson would bark and leap around uncontrollably if he saw another dog, and Lorraine did not dare let him off the leash. She was seriously considering finding another home for him, when a friend suggested that she take him to Keith Davis for training.

The solution • In assessing Samson, Keith discovered that he had not been socialized with dogs and other animals properly, so he recommended socialization classes where Samson could meet other well-behaved and non-reactive dogs in a controlled environment.

Having an expert at hand to show her what to do helped Lorraine deal with the situation more confidently and correctly than she could on her own. She realized that she had actually been making Samson's behaviour worse by not allowing him to socialize with other dogs.

Once Samson was allowed to meet, greet and play with other dogs, the problem resolved itself. He no longer saw them as potential foes and had no reason to react badly to them.

8 Climbing on furniture

Training him to stay off the furniture

If you don't want your dog to sit on the furniture, set a precedent and don't let him do it in the first place. For example, if he is a cute little puppy or a rescue dog, you may feel that he deserves special privileges at first. After that, he will think it is his right to get on your furniture whenever he likes.

If you want the dog to sit on your lap or beside you, but only when you want him to, you have to set clear rules by teaching him that the only time he's allowed on the furniture is when you are there and invite him to sit with you.

1 If your dog won't get off the furniture when you command him to, hook your finger into his collar to take control and say 'off'.

2 If the dog still won't move, gently but firmly remove him, repeating the command 'off'. If he tries to jump back on, sharply command 'no'. If he tries again, again say no and put him out of the room. Let him back in a short time later and tell him to lie down; if he tries to get back on the furniture put him out of the room again. He will learn that getting on the furniture is unrewarding (he is put of the room), while by not doing so, he is allowed to remain in the room with you.

3 To keep your dog off furniture when you cannot monitor him, put obstacles in the way to prevent him from jumping up.

TRAINER'S TIP

With a persistent offender or when re-training, keep the dog away from furniture by using a stair gate. This way, he can still see what's going on and won't feel isolated, while being prevented from getting on furniture.

Key points

- Let your dog on the furniture only if you invite him.

- If you are not there, stop the dog jumping on furniture by restricting his access to it, with a stair gate, closed door(s) or obstacles.

- Every member of the household must not let the dog on the furniture, or he will be confused.

- If the dog approaches a sofa or chair with the intent of jumping up, command 'no' and be sure he obeys.

- When you first acquire your dog, decide what the rules about his being on the furniture will be. You may regret ever allowing him on the sofa when the novelty has worn off and the upholstery is covered with dog hair.

Case history: furniture fanatic

The dog • Bess was a large, two-year-old part-bred German Shepherd. Paul had owned her since she was nine months old, and in the first few weeks of living with him, she had been ill. Succumbing to her soulful eyes, Paul had allowed her to sleep in his bedroom until she recovered.

The problem • Paul did not realize what a problem he was allowing to develop. It wasn't long before Bess began to climb on to the bed during the night. Eventually she claimed the sofa downstairs as well, and no one could sit on it if Bess was *in situ*.

The solution • Trainer Keith Davis was called in to help. After assessing the situation, he concluded that Bess had taken control of the household and was taking as much advantage of this as possible. He advised Paul to ignore her when she came to him for attention, thereby relegating her to second place and reinstating himself as the pack leader. She was also banned from the bedroom.

Keith also suggested introducing Bess to an indoor crate (see pages 44–45) as a place she could call her own and in which she could feel secure. This was done, and she accepted it almost immediately. When she was put in the crate that first night, she objected at first but soon discovered that whining for attention brought no results. A couple of nights later, Bess had settled into her new routine without a fuss.

At this point, the crate door was left open overnight. Paul placed small items of furniture on the sofa and chairs so that Bess could not climb onto them. This strategy also worked.

The next step was to remove the crate but keep the obstacles on the furniture overnight to reduce Bess's habit of climbing on it. Gradually, over a few weeks, she became less and less inclined to seek out furniture on which to lie, and Paul stopped restricting her access to it. She did not return to her old habits.

9 Begging and fussy eating

Dogs who beg at the table and/or are fussy eaters generally have one thing in common – they have been allowed to get away with this behaviour.

The two also tend to go hand in hand because dogs who are given human food seem to prefer it above all else. This is because dogs are instinctively scavengers and also because that is what their human pack leaders eat.

In rare cases, fussy eating can indicate an underlying medical problem, so if the dog has recently started to turn his nose up at whatever you feed him and displays symptoms such as digestive disturbances, skin ailments, rapid weight loss and poor coat condition, take him to the vet for an examination to make sure he is not allergic to the food he is being given.

Dog food, whether wet, semi-moist or dry, can go 'off', which can make it unappetizing for your dog, so always follow the storage instructions on the can or package. Avoid buying a large bag of food unless you are able to use it quickly once it has been opened or can transfer it into airtight containers. Finally, always check the sell-by date on the packaging.

Begging
To deter begging at the table, there are several steps you can take.

• Remove the dog from the room while you are preparing food and eating.

• If your dog responds to being sent away to lie down and stay, then do this every time the family sits down to eat. Make sure everyone in the household is aware of and abides by the rule of not giving the dog human food titbits, since this will encourage him to beg.

• Steel yourself not to give in to your dog's pleading expression and soulful eyes. Insist that he go away from the table and not come harassing you for food.

If your dog fully understands his place at the bottom of your family pack, try feeding him at the same time you have your own meal so he has something to distract him. Follow the rules for feeding explained on page 85. It's a good idea to insist that he lie down quietly after eating while you finish your meal.

Training him to eat what he's given

1 Measure out your dog's ration for the morning then split it in half. Do the same with the evening meal if he is fed twice a day.

2 Put down half of the food for the dog.

3 If he eats it within a few minutes, put down the other half.

4 After 20 minutes, remove any uneaten food and throw it away. Do not give the dog any other food, including treats, until his next mealtime. Be sure that he has a constant supply of fresh, clean water.

Curing a fussy eater

Once your vet has established that your dog is not ill and the food you are providing is suitable for his needs, follow this method and he will be eating up his food within a week. He will learn that the food he is given is all he is going to get, and since dogs won't allow themselves to go hungry, the problem will be solved!

Key points

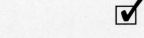

- Do not hand-feed your dog titbits in an effort to get him to eat. It is not necessary and will simply make him even fussier.

- Be sure that no one else in the family gives him titbits, either from the table or between meals.

- Do not keep changing your dog's food in an effort to encourage him to eat. Provided your vet says it is suitable, keep him on the same diet.

- Never leave uneaten food so the dog can help himself whenever he feels like it. Be strict: remove the food so he learns that he either eats when you let him, or goes hungry until the next mealtime.

- Vary the times of day that you feed your dog so he never knows when he will next be fed. This will give him an incentive to eat the food he is given when it is given.

10 Chewing

Dogs who chew things they shouldn't can soon wreck a house, so it's essential to put a stop to this destructive behaviour swiftly.

Dogs chew for a number of reasons:

- To help them teethe (in the case of young dogs)
- Because they are bored
- Because it gives them pleasure

In all cases, the result for the dog is rewarding, so you must provide him with an alternative that is just as rewarding for him and more acceptable to you, while reinforcing the lesson that the dog can chew only certain items that you provide for that purpose.

Restricted access

During re-training, when you are unable to keep an eye on your dog (such as when you are out or are busy elsewhere in the house), restrict him to an area of the house in which he cannot do much, if any, damage (and certainly where there are no accessible electrical wires). Provide him with a chew toy that he can demolish or an activity toy such as a filled Kong (see page 31) to keep him occupied. If there is no suitable area in the house, use a crate (see pages 44–45).

Key points

- Never encourage your dog to pull or chew at clothing during play sessions. This can lead to inappropriate chewing and also to aggressive, dominant behaviour and, ultimately, biting.

- Do not give the dog items of old clothing or discarded shoes to play with or he will view all clothing or shoes, unwanted or not, as fair game.

- Never allow your dog to chew sticks or lumps of wood, since he may not differentiate between that and your table legs. In addition, wood splinters can cause serious injury, and dogs have also become impaled on sticks.

- A bored dog will find his own entertainment, so always provide him with suitable playthings.

- Spray items that your dog persists in chewing with a non-toxic, bitter-tasting anti-chew liquid, available from pet stores.

Teaching him that chewing is unrewarding

1 Have a number of rattle pots – lidded containers half-filled with pebbles or large dry beans – accessible around the house to use when you see your dog chewing inappropriately.

2 Throw a rattle pot so it lands near the dog (obviously, don't aim to hit him!) to interrupt the chewing. As it lands, the dog will stop chewing or jump away in surprise. If you don't feel confident about your aim, or you have a very nervous dog, simply rattle the pot hard instead.

3 Quickly replace the item that he is chewing with a toy or chew treat that the dog can nibble on instead. Encourage him to take it and chew it.

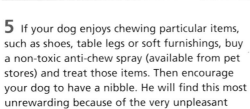

4 Give the dog an activity toy filled with something tasty to keep him occupied, especially if you are busy, so he doesn't get bored and go looking for something inappropriate to chew for entertainment.

5 If your dog enjoys chewing particular items, such as shoes, table legs or soft furnishings, buy a non-toxic anti-chew spray (available from pet stores) and treat those items. Then encourage your dog to have a nibble. He will find this most unrewarding because of the very unpleasant taste and won't be likely to try it again.

TRAINER'S TIP

It is a two-fold problem when your dog grabs the mail as the postman is putting it through the letterbox and then rips it to shreds. To solve this quickly and easily, either put a separate mailbox outside your front door or attach a wire drop box to the door over the letterbox so the mail is protected when it drops through.

11 Door manners

A dog who pushes past his owner and rushes to
the door when someone calls is a real nuisance. Not only
could this result in an accident if you trip over him, but
people could become reluctant to visit if they know they
are going to be jumped all over when they enter the house.
Few people like an ill-mannered dog.

Use the reward container technique (see
pages 68–69) whenever someone comes
to the door. Your dog will soon learn
that going to his designated place and
staying there when visitors knock is more
rewarding than rushing to the door to
greet them. Do remember to reward
your dog for correct behaviour.
Eventually this becomes a conditioned
response, and you will need to use treats
only occasionally; verbal praise will be
sufficient the rest of the time.

There are a number of things you can do
to either prevent or re-train this
behaviour. If your house layout allows it,
put a see-through gate across the hall to
deny your dog access to the door. Once
your visitors are inside, they should
ignore the dog until he settles down,
then say hello to him.

Teaching him good door manners

1 Enlist another person to help you practise this exercise with your pushy dog; also, review 'sit' and 'stay' training (see pages 62–63 and 66–67). When a visitor comes to the door, command your dog to sit and stay before you open it.

2 Greet your visitor and tell her to ignore the dog until you decide to call him over to say hello. Don't wait too long at first, because if the dog's excitement gets the better of him and he ignores your stay command, it may set the training back a step. If the dog does approach without your permission, tell your visitor to ignore him until he has settled down and you can reinstate the 'sit-stay' position.

3 Reinforcing the 'sit-stay' command, let your visitor greet the dog, but instruct her to ignore him if he rushes over or jumps up. Once the dog has been greeted, you can either let him stay with you and the visitor or send him to lie down quietly again. Constant reinforcement of this exercise will soon teach the required response when someone comes to the door. The dog learns that rushing to the door is unrewarding, while not doing so results in pleasant interaction with guests.

Key points

- If your dog is uncontrollable at the door, ensure his safety and that of your visitors by putting him securely in another room.

- Remember that *you* are the pack leader in your home, not your dog, so don't let him greet visitors before you do.

- Command your dog to sit and stay before attaching the leash to take him for a walk.

- Never allow your dog to push through a door before you. Make him wait, even if it takes several minutes to reinforce by using the door-shutting exercise (see pages 122–3). Add the command 'wait' to the exercise as your dog does so, and reward him when he complies.

- Continual, consistent command reinforcement is the only way to teach your dog what you require of him.

Pushing through doors

Does this look familiar? Curing this habit is quite simple when you know how. You will need someone to act as a caller at the door, then you can implement the re-training procedure.

Teaching him to wait

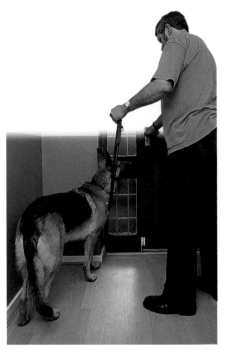

1 Put the dog on a leash and stand by the door, waiting for your assistant to knock or ring. When he does, open the door a little way.

 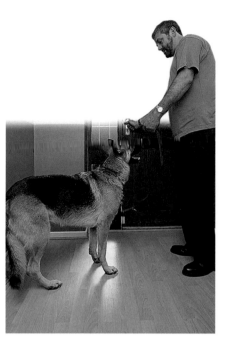  

2 At this point, the dog will try to barge through to see who is there.

3 When he does, slam the door shut (being careful not to trap his nose) and the dog will jump back in surprise.

4 Practise this a few times until the dog doesn't try to push past you when someone knocks and you open the door, but instead stands quietly, watching and waiting to see what you are going to do next. He has discovered that pushing past you is unpleasant, because the door is shut in his face.

5 Next, command your dog to 'sit' and 'stay' as you open the door. When he does, reward him. He will learn that waiting while you answer the door is more pleasant than trying to push through it. Gradually, you can work towards opening the door wider each time. The next step is to teach your dog to remain in the sit-stay while guests enter, as explained on pages 120–121.

12 Travel problems

Dogs who are reactive in the car – barking, jumping about, soiling or vomiting – are generally this way because the sight of the world going by upsets them and the vehicle's motion makes them feel queasy.

In addition, if you only ever take your dog in the car to the vet's surgery for treatment, he will associate the vehicle with something unpleasant and is likely to be unsettled while in transit.

Car safety

Do not let your dog jump out of the car until you are sure it is safe, both for him and for others. If your dog insists on barging his way out regardless, you need to re-train him.

Some dogs respond well to a travel harness. Make sure it fits comfortably and correctly – snugly enough that he can't escape, but not so tightly that it causes discomfort.

Key points ✓

- Never let your dog travel unsecured in a vehicle. It is not safe for either the dog or the driver and passengers.

- Do not let your dog jump out of the car before you are ready for him to do so.

- If you are travelling with your dog in a crate, cover it so he cannot see anything at which to bark.

- Attaching a long leash to the dog's collar or headcollar and tugging on it, simultaneously saying 'no', may help stop reactive behaviour in the car.

- When getting the dog in and out of the car, vary your timing: don't always let him jump straight in or out but do it when you are ready.

- Putting a headcollar on a dog when transporting him can help to improve his behaviour by giving him something to think about other than reacting to anything he sees.

- When your dog is in transit, drive smoothly, especially around corners. Get your dog used to travelling by taking only short trips at first.

Put a reactive dog in a travel crate (some indoor crates can also be used in vehicles) to transport him. (See pages 44–45 for how to crate train your dog.) Put the dog's blanket in with him for familiarity, along with his favourite toy and an activity toy to keep him occupied and distracted. Cover the crate with a sheet or blanket; if the dog cannot see out, he cannot see anything to which he could react. Covering the crate has a calming effect and is well worth trying.

1 When you start to open the door, the dog will come close to it with his head down, ready to leap out.

2 As he does, close the door, and the dog will leap back in surprise. Keep repeating this exercise until he stays away from the door as you open it.

3 Attach the leash securely, tell the dog to sit or stay, and reward him.

4 Once you are satisfied that it is safe, let the dog out and tell him to come to heel and sit so you can close the door and lock the car. Practise this every time you take the dog out of the car.

Case history: terrier travel

The dog • Missy was a small terrier type, 18 months old. Her owner, Doreen, had brought her home from a rescue centre three weeks earlier.

The problem • When travelling in the car, Missy barked at anything and everything she saw. She was free to sit where she wanted, and she ended up jumping from seat to seat in order to get a better vantage point from which to bark. She could – and did – 'chase' a dog, passer-by or cyclist through 360 degrees around the inside of the car! Doreen could not cope with Missy's behaviour any longer: it was 'cure or go back' time.

The solution • Keith Davis explained to Doreen that the best way to deal with a problem of this type is to secure the dog in the car in a travel harness or crate, in the rear of an estate vehicle or on the back seat of a saloon. Doreen had a crate, so Keith showed her how to position it in the car. He then advised her to give Missy an activity toy to keep her occupied and to cover the crate with a blanket. He explained that if the dog could not see anything to bark at, she wouldn't bark.

Keith's advice worked: Doreen still has Missy, who now travels contentedly and quietly in the covered crate.

INDEX

ACKNOWLEDGEMENTS

Executive Editor Trevor Davies
Executive Art Editor Leigh Jones
Editor Katy Denny
Designer Jo Tapper
Picture Researcher Jennifer Veall
Production Controller Ian Paton
Photographer Angus Murray